Blues Harmonica

BY Tommy Morgan

A Complete Manual for Beginners and Professionals

Tommy Morgan, harmonicist, recording artist, concert artist, and composer is a native of Los Angeles. Morgan has recorded more than 200 feature films, countless radio and television commercials and numerous television series and specials. He has also been an arranger for Glen Yarborough, Rod McKuen, and Johnny Cash.

Tommy first recorded with the Andrews Sisters in 1950. Since then, he has given four command performances as a concert artist, and has soloed with symphony orchestras and concert bands throughout the world.

In 1961, Morgan returned to UCLA where he had earlier earned a Bachelor of Science degree in accounting. This time Morgan received a Masters in music composition and returned to the Hollywood recording scene as a composer. Morgan has recorded for television specials "Roots," "Centennial," "The Autobiography of Miss Pitman," "The Elvis Presley Special," and "The Blue and The Grey." In addition, Morgan has written scores for episodes of "The Twilight Zone" and "Gunsmoke." He has recorded with the Beach Boys, Dean Martin, Andy Williams, Neil Diamond, The Carpenters, Barbra Streisand, Tony Tenille, Henry Mancini, Lalo Schifrin, Linda Ronstadt and is heard on many Motown hit records. It is also his harmonica you hear on television programs such as "Green Acres," "Sanford and Son," "The Rockford Files," "The Waltons," and "Gunsmoke," to name a few. In the movies his harmonica virtuosity is ever present in films such as "Lilies of the Field," "Cool Hand Luke," "Patch of Blue," "Cincinnati Kid," "The Wild Bunch," "Cat Balou," and "The Color Purple." Although Morgan rarely makes personal appearances, you can catch a glimpse of him performing on Linda Ronstadt's video release of "Skylark," and her "Lush Life" album which was released in 1985.

Tommy Morgan currently resides in Southern California with his wife and two college-age sons, where he has been a church choir director since 1968. He is also a record-holding glider pilot with over 20 years of experience, and holds a Second-Degree Black Belt in Hapkido Karate.

TOMMY MORGAN BLUES HARMONICA
by Tommy Morgan

CONTENTS

FOREWORD

Hollywood studio musicians have to be the most versatile performers in the world because of the great variety of demands made upon them. My friend Tommy Morgan is outstanding among this top echelon of players. He can turn on the "grease" at a wild rhythm and blues session for Motown in the afternoon; and then put on his tuxedo and play the Villa-Lobos Concerto for Harmonica that same night at the Hollywood Bowl with the symphony. Brother, that's musicianship!

Besides being one of the most versatile harmonica virtuosos in the world, Tommy's background as a scholar and composer, (Masters Degree in Music Composition, UCLA; composer of numerous movie and TV scores) uniquely qualifies him to write this book on the harmonica. Tommy has much to give. You and I are lucky – we have much to gain.

HUGO MONTENEGRO

INTRODUCTION

The title of this book, "BLUES HARMONICA", is used to describe the style of playing associated with Blues and Rock music. The instrument used is the Diatonic Harmonica. There are other types of harmonicas, and they are explained in the book, "TOMMY MORGAN – CHROMATIC HARMONICA". This book is about the Diatonic Harmonica, and how it is used and played in today's Blues, Rock and Country music.

This book was written to provide a sound basis for the beginning student, and a clearer understanding for the intermediate and advanced student of just what the Diatonic Harmonica is, what it can do, and how to do it. The step-by-step approach is ideally suited for any level: for the person who has never played before, the pictures and text show you exactly how to hold the instrument and play a single note; for the intermediate player who wants to brush up on the basics and then improve his playing for fun and at his own pace; and for the advanced player who wants to improve his playing and to learn the style and how to play many of the figures and solos in today's music.

Whether you're learning something new, want just to have fun and sound better for yourself and your friends, or are really "getting into it" as a player, this book will answer your questions and will help you learn and enjoy the harmonica.

There is a Cassette available that demonstrates this book (Item 3340).

TOMMY MORGAN

Chapter One

The Diatonic Harmonica

The Diatonic Harmonica is an instrument that produces its tone by pushing a column of air past a metal reed, causing it to vibrate, and thus to "sound". It has an incomplete scale -- no sharps or flats. For example, in the key of C, only the white notes on the piano can be played, and even a few of these are missing (see Page 6). It sounds limited, but in the hands of a good player, many of these "missing" notes may be played by changing the pitch of those notes that are on the instrument (see Page 14). This "bending" of the notes is the sound so often heard in Blues, Rock and some Country music.

There are a number of different types and models of harmonicas. The most popular is the 10 hole, and the most famous, the Hohner Marine Band. This and certain of the other 10 hole models are made in all 12 keys. All of the information in this book will deal with the Marine Band Harmonicas, and will be true for almost all of the diatonic instruments made. After reading this material, I'm sure that you will be able to recognize the differences in the other types of Diatonic Harmonicas and readily adapt to them.

How To Hold The Harmonica

Hold the harmonica in the Left Hand, numbered side up. This puts the low notes to the left, like a piano.* The entire weight is held between the index finger and the thumb. The other fingers do not rest on the instrument. The harmonica rests in the "V" formed at the base of the thumb and index finger.

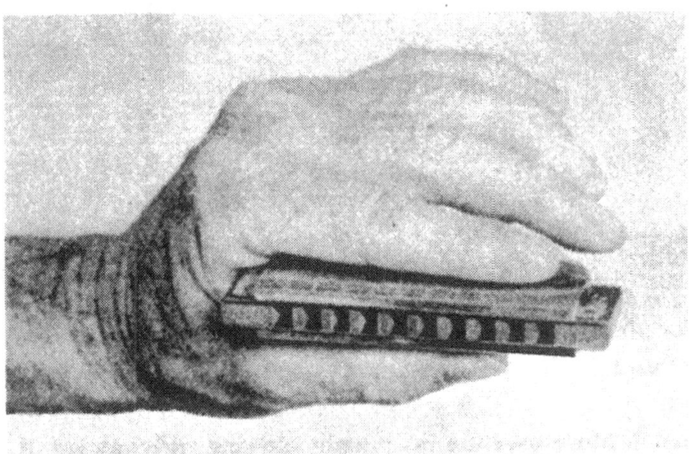

** If you already play the harmonica and have been holding it the other way — numbered side down and in the Right Hand, don't change. Go ahead with the way you've been doing it, unless you're just starting. Simply reverse the directions. There are some very good players who do play it "backwards".*

The Right Hand is cupped around the Left, forming a tone chamber. The thumbs are parallel along the bottom. Remember, the weight is supported entirely by the LEFT Hand.

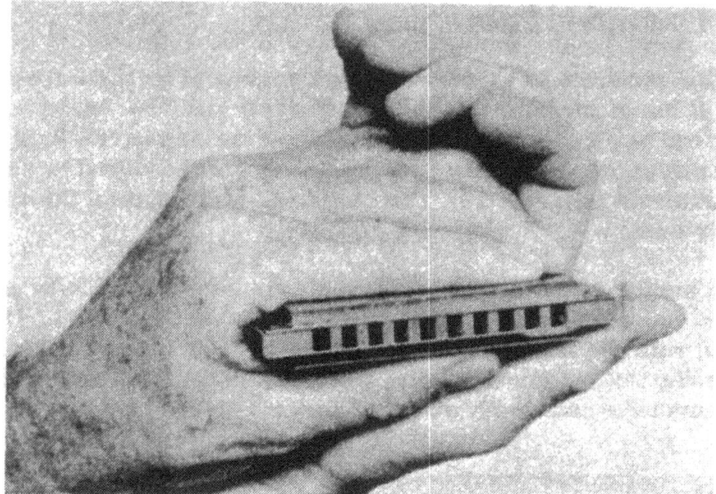

Open the Right Hand part way. This is the ½ open position

How To Play A Single Note

There are two ways to play a single note – Lipping and Tongue Blocking. Lipping is most often used. Not only is it easier to "bend" the notes (see Page 14), it also frees the tongue for use in rhythm playing and special effects (see Page 19). I suggest that you start with the Lipping method.

LIPPING: Purse the lips to form a hole the size of the hole in the mouthpiece. Place your lips on the mouthpiece in middle of the instrument and blow.

Lips Pursed

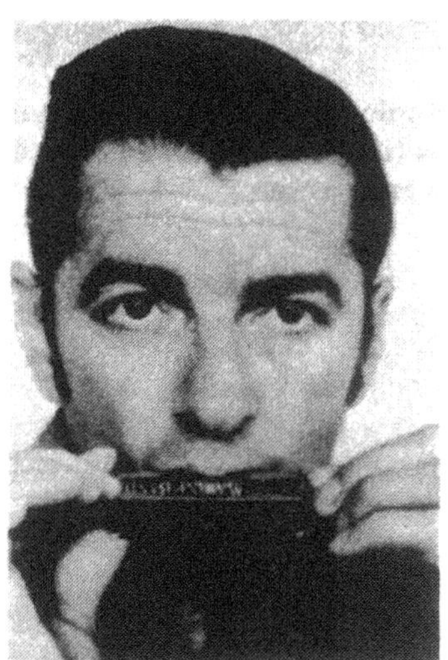

Lips on Harmonica

Now try a draw note (inhale). Move over the instrument blowing and drawing. If you are getting more than one note, make the lips form a smaller hole. If you're getting one note but it is very "pinched" sounding and hard to blow, let the lips form a slightly larger hole.

You will find that it is harder to produce a good clear tone with some of the high and low notes. If these sound bad and flat, don't worry about the instrument. Chances are it's you. Don't worry about you either. This will resolve itself with practice and learning to play with the mouth relaxed.

TONGUE BLOCKING. Spread your lips slightly and place the harmonica into your mouth. The right side of your mouth should be about in the middle of the mouthpiece (it's easier to start here). Your lips will cover 3 or 4 holes. Don't stretch or pinch your lips. Place the tongue lightly on the mouthpiece, leaving one hole open between the right side of the tongue and the right corner of the mouth. Try not to jam your tongue into the mouthpiece. Blow into the harmonica.

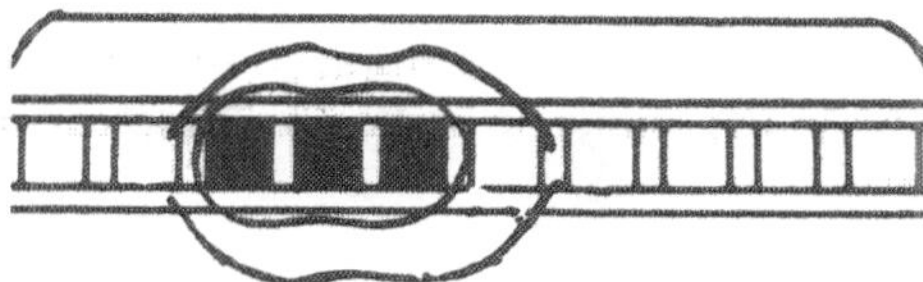

Chances are your first attempt will feel awkward, and won't sound very good. Try again, only this time move the harmonica up to your mouth, and not into it. Put your tongue on the mouthpiece, move the harmonica a little to the left without letting your tongue slide over, place it in your mouth and blow. You will notice that your lips have a tendency to push forward and point.

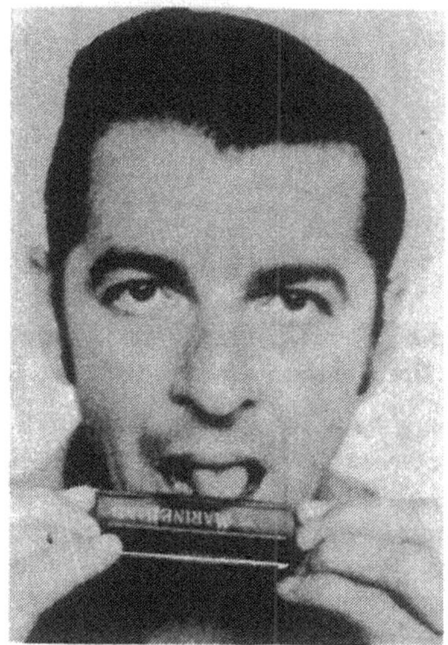

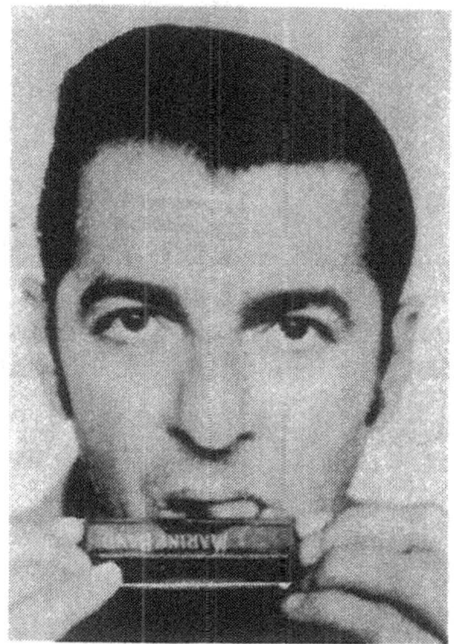

Move over the instrument blowing and drawing. Try for a good clear tone. As with Lipping, some of the high and low notes will be hard to play.

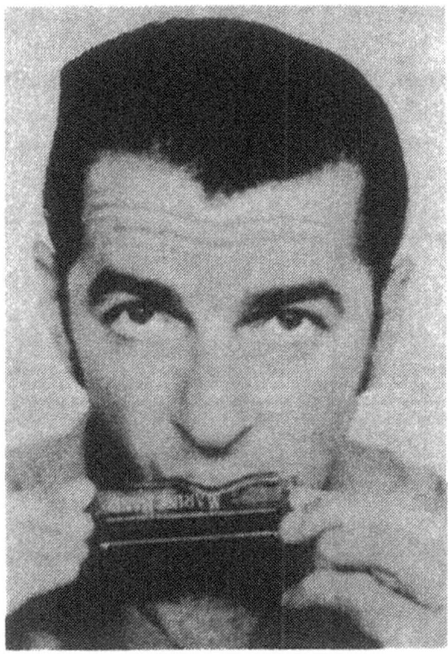

The Notes On The Harmonica

The Diatonic Harmonica is made in all 12 keys. The use of harmonicas in different keys is explained on Page 26. For our illustrations we will use a harmonica made in the key of C – a C Harmonica.

Blow into hole #4. This note is C. To be sure that you have the right hole (you can't see the numbers when you're playing), take the harmonica in both hands in front of you and put your left index finger in hole #3 and your right index finger in hole #5. Bring the harmonica as close to your mouth as possible and blow between your fingers.

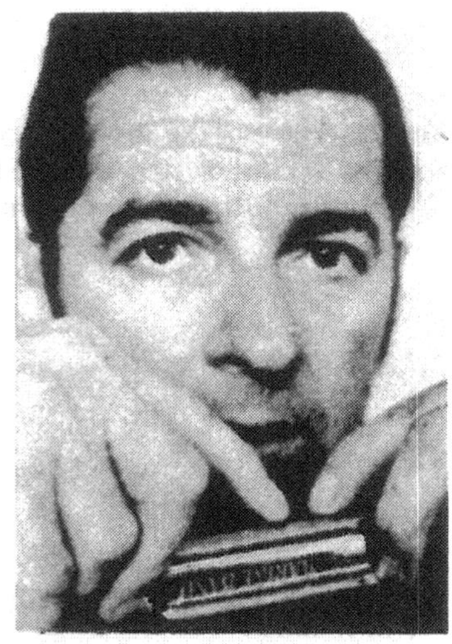

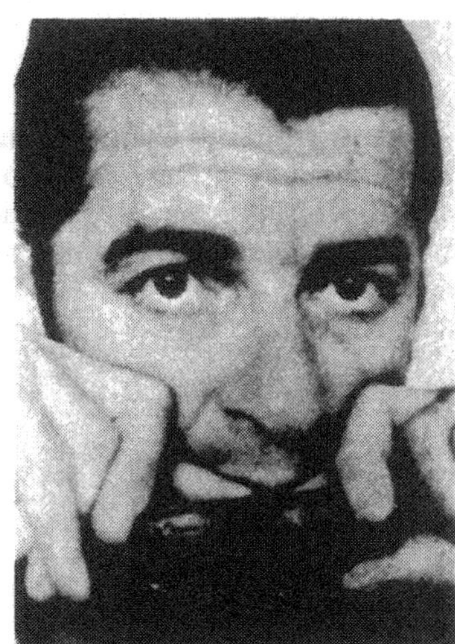

Listen to the note. Now play hole #4 the correct way — I assume you are Lipping. Same note? If not, try again until you can play hole #4 just by "feel"; without looking at the numbers before you put it in your mouth.

Now draw. This note is D.

Notes of the C scale.

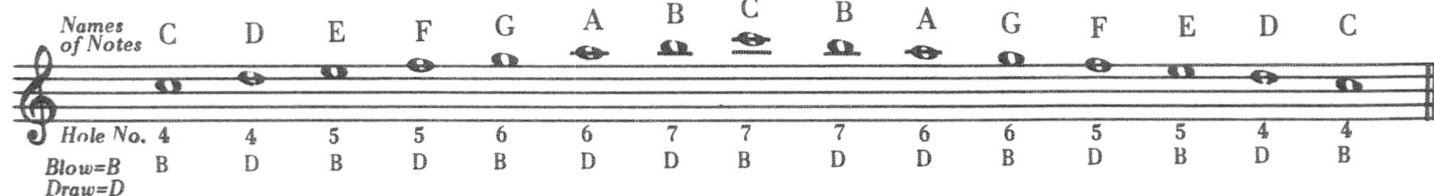

Play the scale up slowly, and then back down. This is just like playing on the white notes of the piano.

The notes on the entire harmonica.

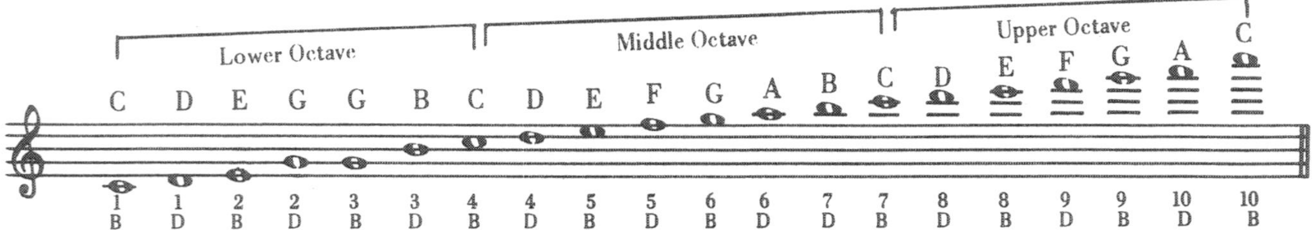

Note the missing F and A in the lower octave, and the missing B in the upper octave. Only the middle octave has a complete diatonic scale. Also note that the G in the lower octave can be played either blow or draw.

All of the exercises include chord symbols. It's more fun to play with accompaniment, so if you have a friend who plays the guitar or piano, have him play along with you. This will also let you hear some of the different chords, and teach you what notes to play with them.

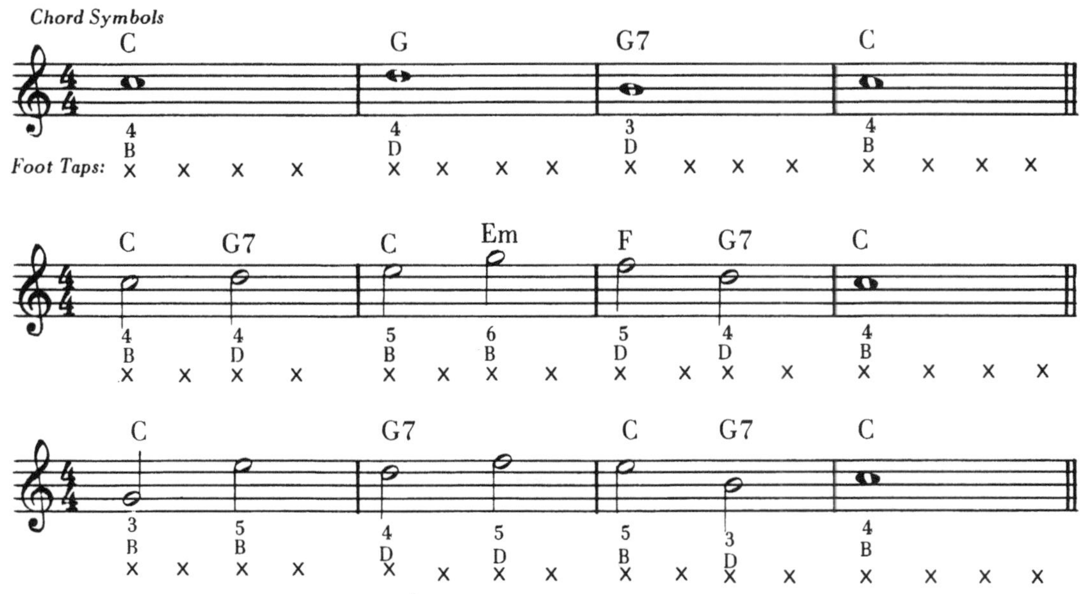

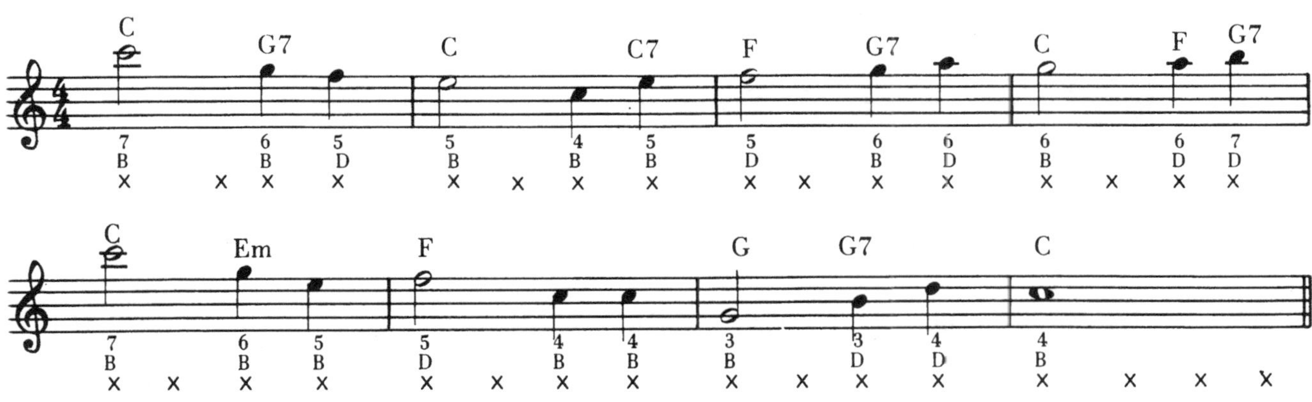

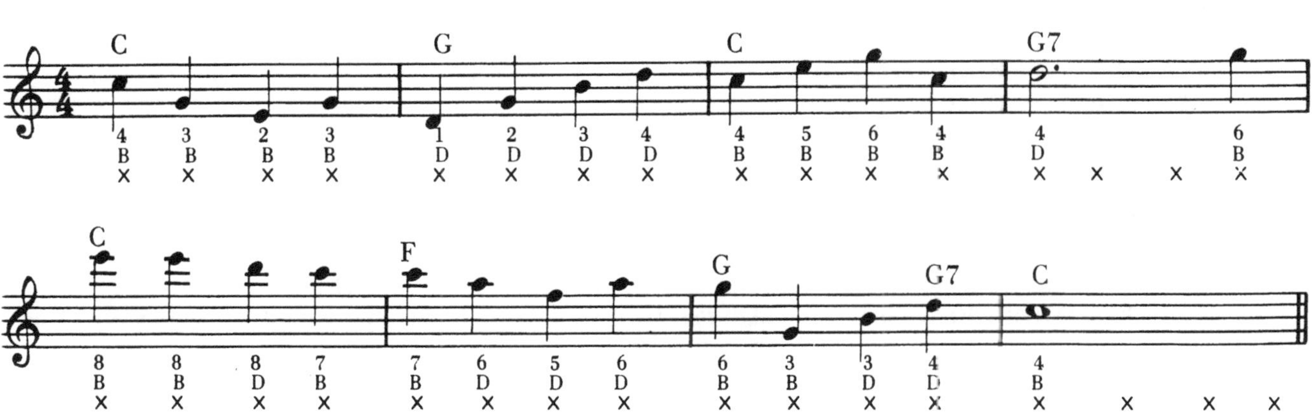

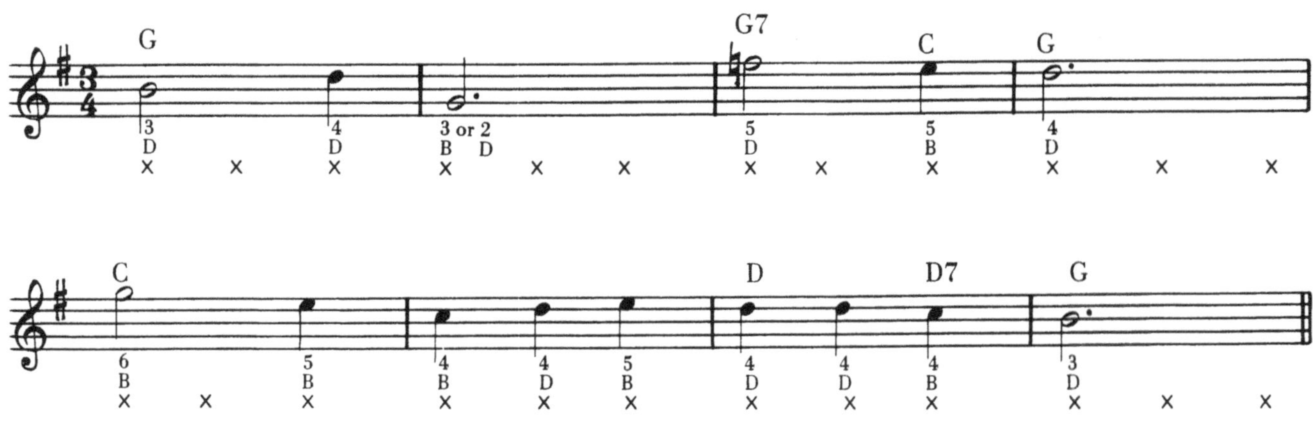

Vibrato

Vibrato (sometimes mistakenly referred to as tremolo) is a wavery quality added to a tone. It should not be used to cover up a poor tone, but rather to enhance an already good sound.

Before adding vibrato, you should be able to play clear, pure tones with good quality. To help do this, practice long tones. Start a note very softly, gradually increase to loud, and then back down to soft and fade away. The crescendo (soft to loud) and decrescendo (loud to soft) should be smooth, with no sudden or jumpy changes. Practice all blow and draw notes.

There are two main types of vibrato — HAND and THROAT.

HAND VIBRATO. This is the most common vibrato, and the one most often heard. The Right Hand is rapidly opened and closed. The thumbs and heels of the hands stay together. It is mostly the fingers that move, and not too far at that. This changes the color and volume of the tone, but does not affect the pitch. The WAH-WAH produced should be smooth and continuous. Be able to play at different speeds.

THROAT VIBRATO. This vibrato changes the pitch of the note. It is not effective in the upper octave. Start by taking a draw note (it's easier to draw than blow). Start the tone by saying AH in the throat. Of course, don't sound it with your vocal chords. This short blast of air flats the note at the beginning, and then it comes up to pitch. Just as the note reaches its correct pitch, AH is said again. The continuous vibrato is made by saying a stream of AHs. These must be evenly spaced and very uniform as to loudness in order to achieve an even and smooth vibrato. It is most effective on the lower half of the harmonica, and with draw notes. It is also easier Lipping than Tongue Blocking. It is effective as a true vibrato only with one note, although it may be used with two or more as a "type" of vibrato or pulse.

THE WAIL. Like the throat vibrato, the Wail changes the pitch of the note. It is most effective in the upper octave with blow notes. The tongue is pulsed to form a vibrato ("saying" something like YOI-YOI-YOI). It sounds like a deep throat vibrato, but in the high register it comes out a "Wailing" sound. Tongue Block rather than Lip.

Chapter Two

How To Play Blues Harmonica

Blues Harmonica, Blues Harp or Harp Style (Harp being short for French Harp — or Mouth Harp — other terms for harmonica) is the style of playing that originated in the South. It is tremendously exciting and creative.

We will be most concerned with improvisation; that is, working around a series of chords and improvising or making up melodies and figures rather than playing the notes of a song all the way through. To be able to play the right notes for the right chords, we must first look at the harmonies or changes (short for chord changes)of the music.

12 Bar Blues

The basic blues structure is the 12 Bar (measure) progression using three different chords in a major key.

Key of C.

C Chord — Tonic chord built on the first or "tonic" note of the scale.

F Chord — Subdominant chord built on the fourth note of the scale.

G Chord — Dominant chord built on the fifth note of the scale. This chord generally has the added 7th (7th note above G, its root) and is written and called a "G Seventh Chord", or just "G Seventh".

The notes in the chords.

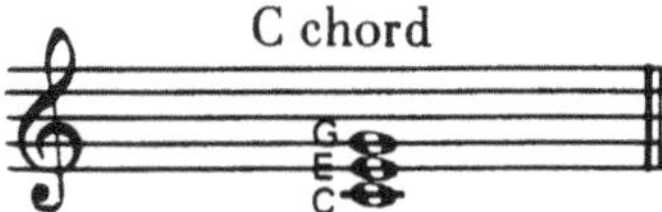

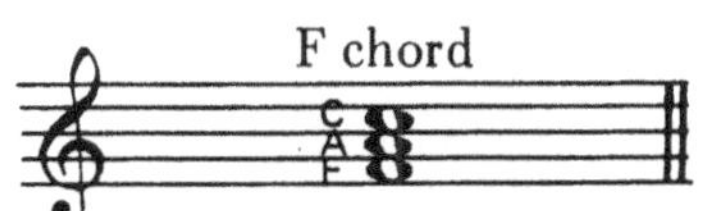

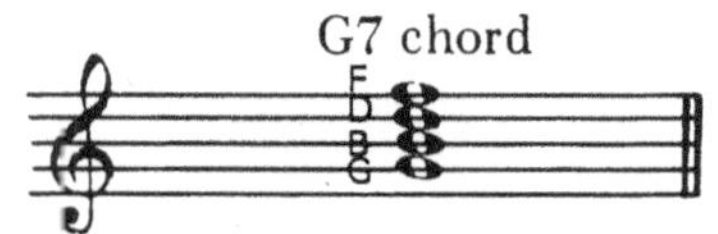

To hear these chords, or to "get them in your head" as they say, have a friend play them on some instrument (guitar or piano).

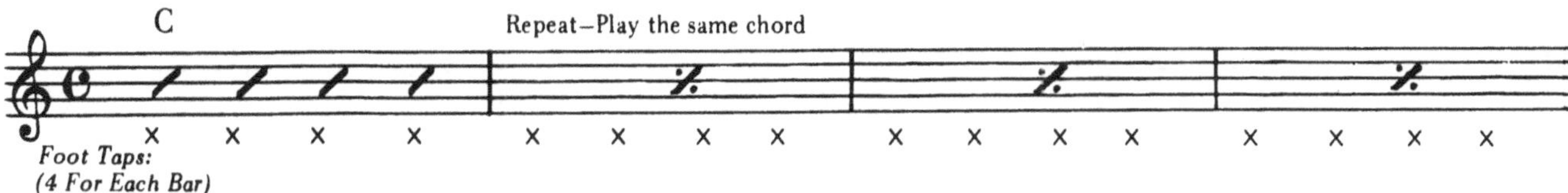

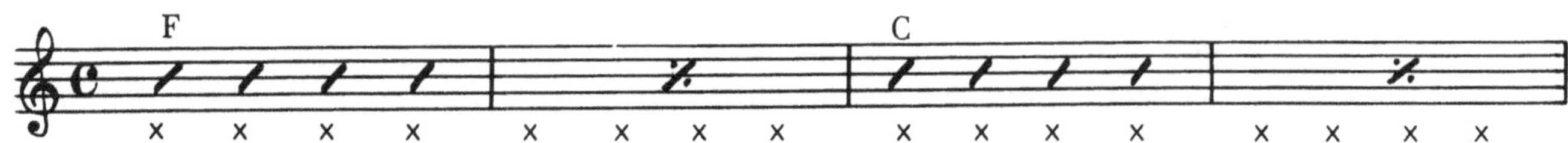

Straight Harp

This is the practice of taking a harmonica and playing it in its own key. To play in the key of C, we use a C Harmonica. The notes on the C Harmonica that fit the various chords in the key of C are:

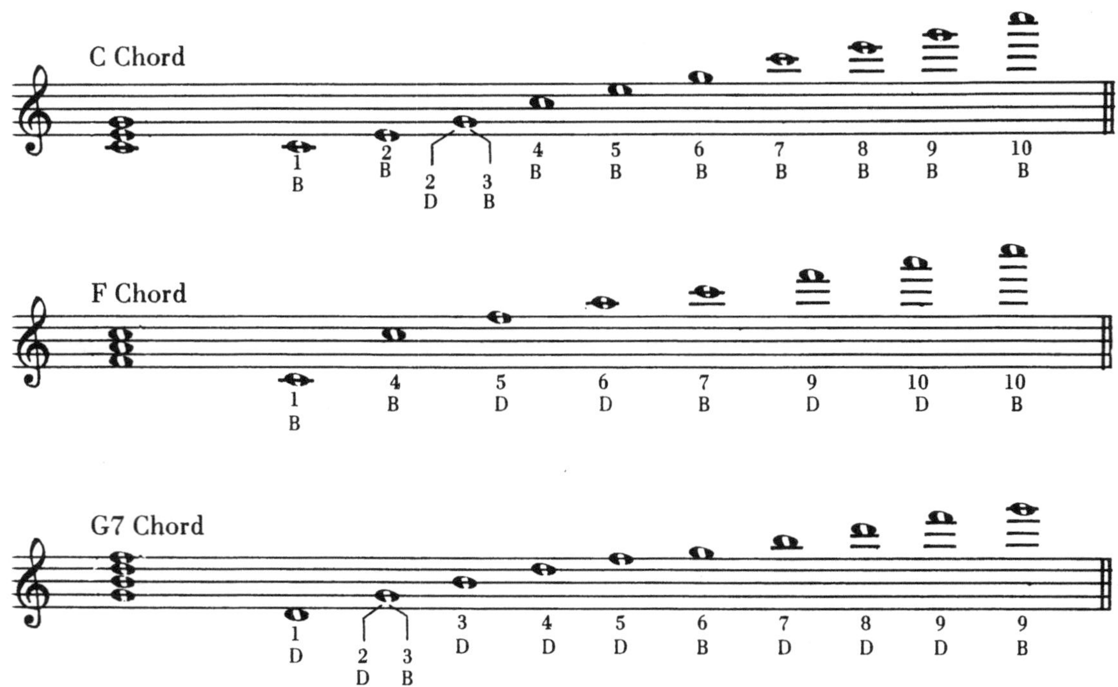

Try all of the notes that fit each chord. Memorize which notes go with what chord.

A solo using only chord tones — the notes that fit each chord.

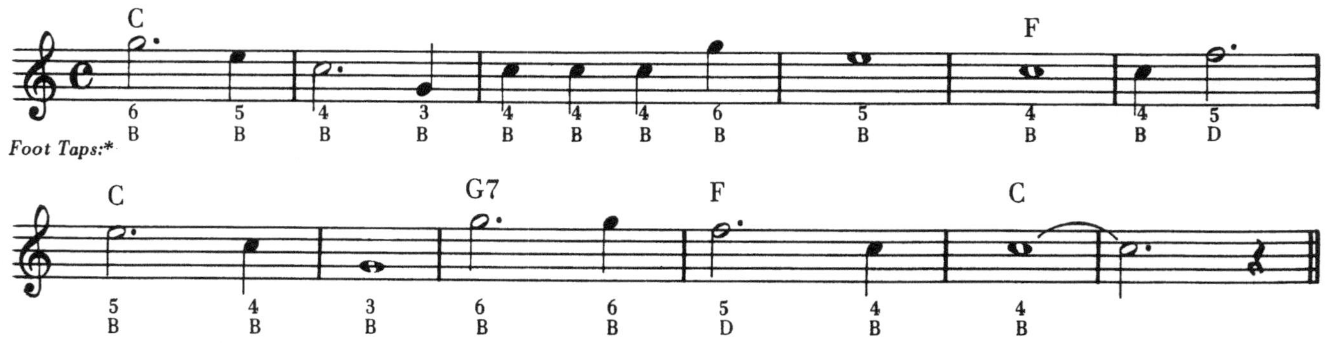

** From this point on, Foot Taps are only marked when a new rhythm is used.*

The notes that fit the chords are not to be considered the only ones to use. The *passing* notes, those notes that are used to pass from one chord tone to another; the *suspensions*, a note starting as a chord tone and held, even though the chord has changed and the note is not a chord tone of the new chord; the *upper and lower neighbors*, the note next to a chord tone that you go to and then back to the same chord tone; and the *added* notes, those notes added to the chords that our ears have become used to, are all what make the great solos, background figures and licks that give music its excitement and life. There is much syncopation (i.e. accenting or stressing notes that don't fall on the beat) both with chord tones and non-chord tones.

Below is a solo using some non-chord tones and some syncopation. Compare this to the example given on the preceding page. It's the same solo, but with the additions just mentioned.

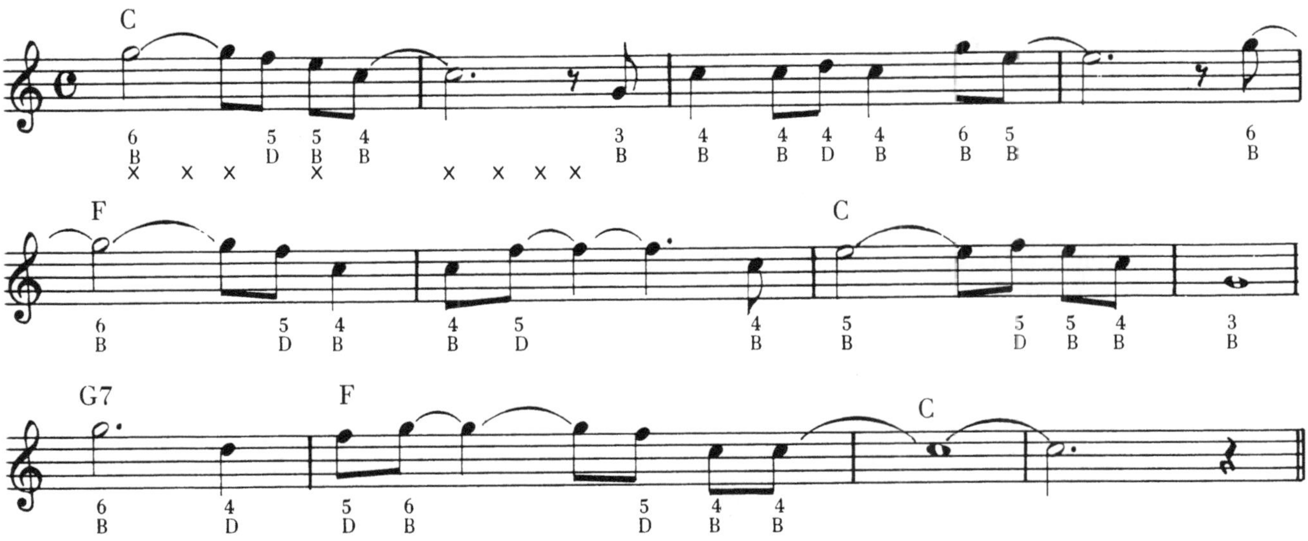

Sometimes a note could be non-chord or something else. The G in the 10th measure with the F chord — upper neighbor or added 9th? Because it lasts so long (2 beats), we consider it the added ninth. If it were written F 1½ beats, G ½ beat, and F 1 beat, it would be considered an upper neighbor.

The most important non-chord tones are:

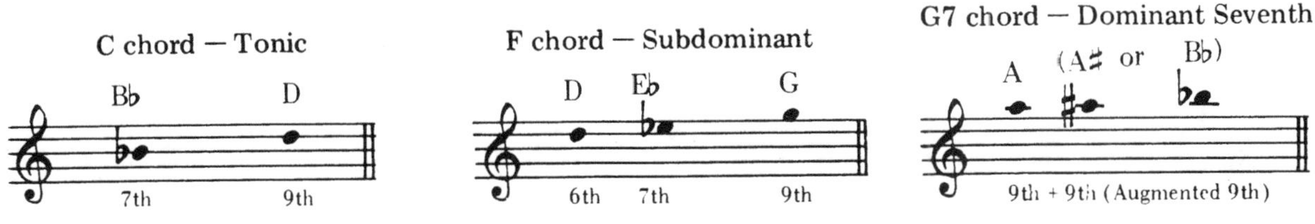

The chord and non-chord tones that may be played.

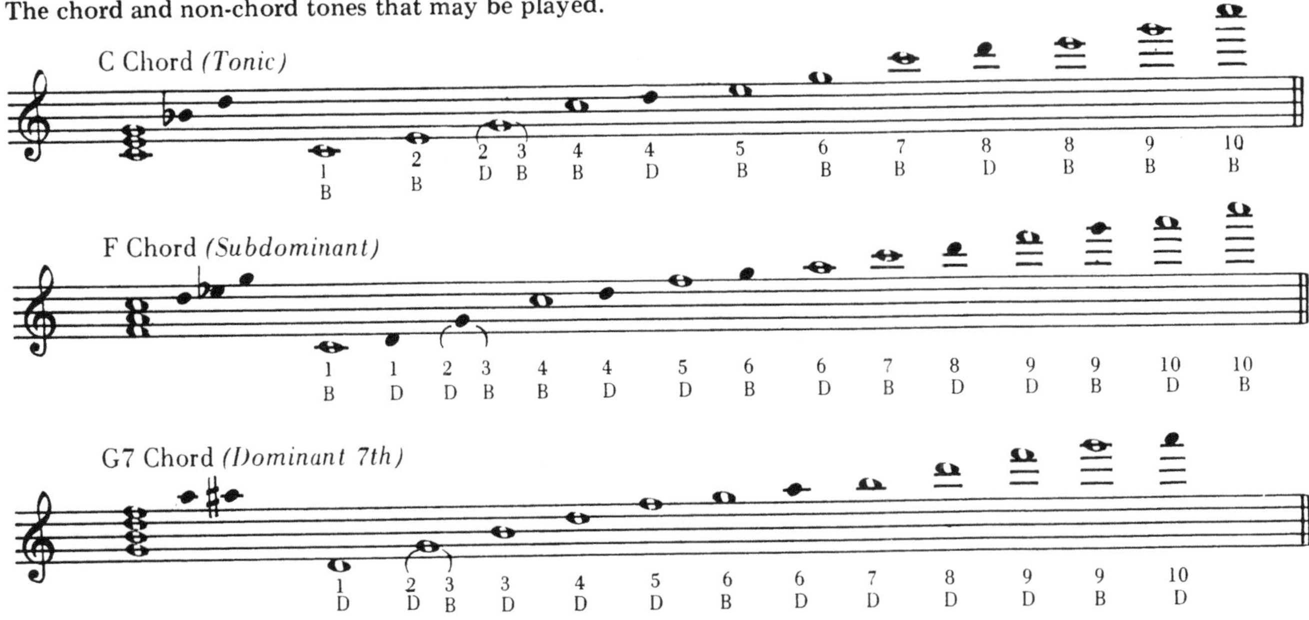

In the above examples, we have used a C Harmonica to play in the key of C. Most players have learned to play another way – Cross Harp.

Cross Harp

This is the practice of taking a harmonica in one key and using it to play in another key. Most of the playing in Blues and Rock and much of the Country playing is done this way.

CROSS HARP — FIRST POSITION. This is the one most often used. With the C Harmonica, you blow a C chord, the tonic. When you draw the first four holes, you get a G chord, the dominant. If you call this G chord your tonic chord, you are now in the Key of G. The three basic chords in the Key of G are: G chord — *Tonic;* C chord — *Subdominant;* D7 chord — *Dominant Seventh.*

The notes in the chords, including the most important non-chord tones.

The chord and non-chord tones that may be played. Remember, we're using a C Harmonica to play in the Key of G.

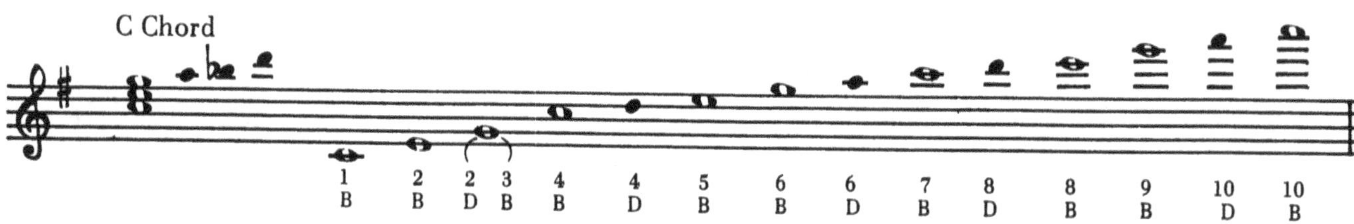

A solo — Key of G/C Harmonica

★ *Two notes together; spread the lips a little wider. These "double stops" are also very much the style of Blues Harmonica.*

Why Cross Harp?

Notice how different the solo above sounds from the Straight Harp solo on Page 11. It "feels" and sounds more like blues.

We used the added 7th for the tonic (F♮ for the G chord). This is the most important added tone for blues, and can't be played Straight Harp (B♭ for the C chord). The ♮9 for the dominant seventh (F♮ for the D7 chord) is also very characteristic and important.

You have now discovered for yourself that except for the high register, the blow notes are "softer" and do not respond nearly as well as the draw. You can hit the draws in the lower two octaves harder, sharper and louder. Most of the solo on Page 13 is played draw. The added ninth for the subdominant chord may be played both Straight Harp (G for the F chord) and Cross Harp (D for the C chord), but it's more effective Cross Harp because it's draw.

Bending Notes

This is the art of lowering the pitch of a note. If you lower it far enough, you can actually produce a note that isn't on the harmonica. You can't raise the pitch of a note.

To bend a note, start by drawing D in hole #4 with a Lipped tone. Now with the mouth, form the syllables WEE-OOO. Note that the tongue drops back away from the teeth on OOO. Draw quite hard. On OOO, the pitch should have dropped. If not, try again. Tighten the lips a little and draw harder at the same time. If that hasn't done it, rest a minute, and try again. Really bite down with the inside of the mouth on OOO.

Another approach. Form the mouth as if you were drinking through a straw. Now just as if the straw was stuck, suck hard on it, with the lips pursed. The pitch should drop. If it drops at all, remember what the mouth feels like, and work at lowering the pitch even more. Let the pitch slide back up to its normal tone. Practice starting with the pitch normal, flatting to the desired note below, and then let it go back up.

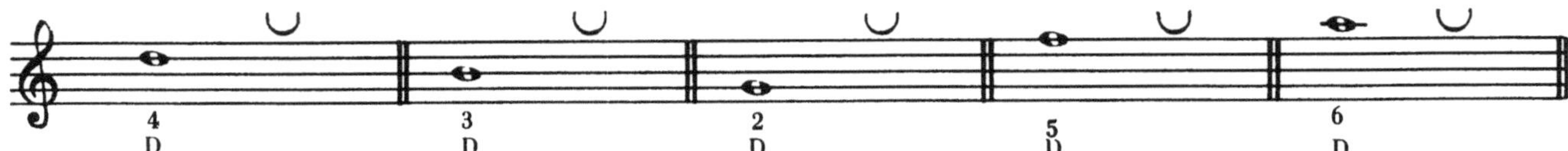

The musical notation for bending a note is ◡.

Practice starting the pitch flat, letting it up to normal, and then back down.

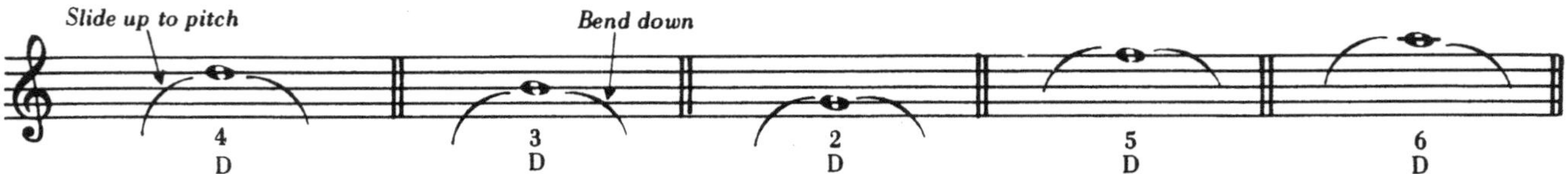

A combination of both of the above.

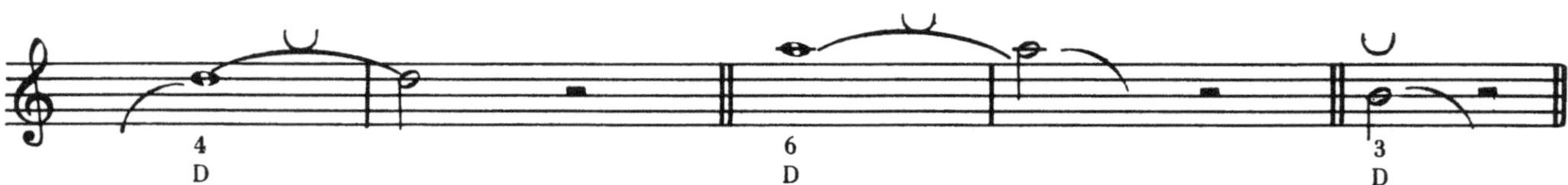

Now try a blow note. Notice how little success you have? In the low and medium octaves, the blow tones will never be as èasy as the draw. At hole #7 blow bending suddenly gets easier and the draw more difficult. For this upper octave, Tongue Blocking works better than Lipping. Experiment. Remember, always strive for control, so that the instrument will do what you want it to do at the right time.

Bending To Create New Notes

The distance between the notes B and C, and E and F is a ½ step. The distance between all of the other notes (white notes on the piano) is a whole step (twice as far). To play the missing F and A in the lower octave, you must lower the pitch twice as far as you do to play the missing ½ steps (the sharps and flats — black notes on the piano) in the middle octave. These missing notes are marked(●).

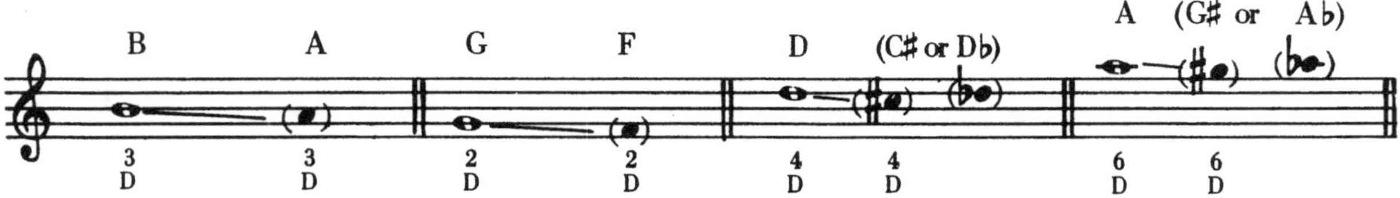

The blow notes are extremely difficult to bend. Work at it, but don't be discouraged.

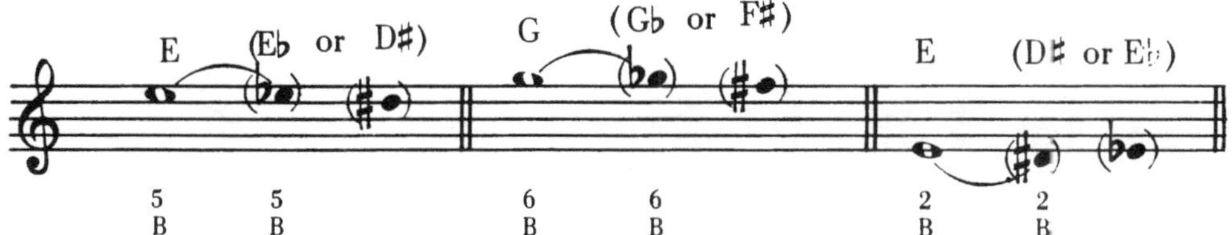

Try the upper octave.

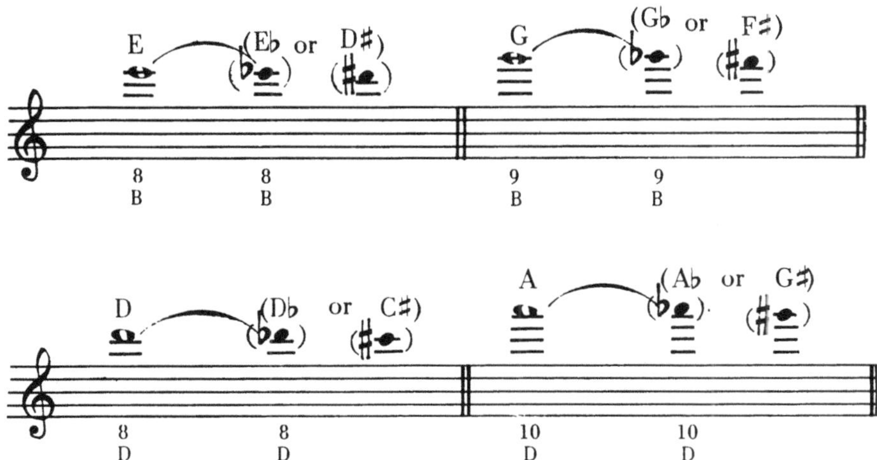

Practice sliding from one note to the other, starting at pitch and bending down, and then back up.

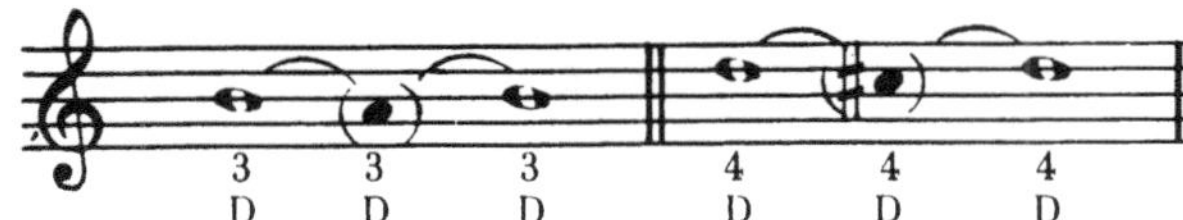

Practice starting from the lowered note, sliding up to the "natural" note, and then back down.

Try going directly from one note to another so that they sound like two separate notes, not one sliding into the other. The small "break" is achieved by moving the mouth quickly from the normal to the flat position, or from the flat to the normal. To help get this little break, as you shift the mouth, say TAH with the tongue. This stops the air momentarily at the first pitch, the mouth quickly shifts, and the next note is started cleanly with the tongue.

When starting a lowered note, it will start cleaner with TAH than just drawing.

When a note or a pattern of notes is repeated, the hole number – B or D – marking will usually not be repeated. You should be looking more at the notes than the numbers. Use the numbers only to get started if you forget the note itself.

Try bending double stops — two notes together. It takes more effort and air, but is very effective.

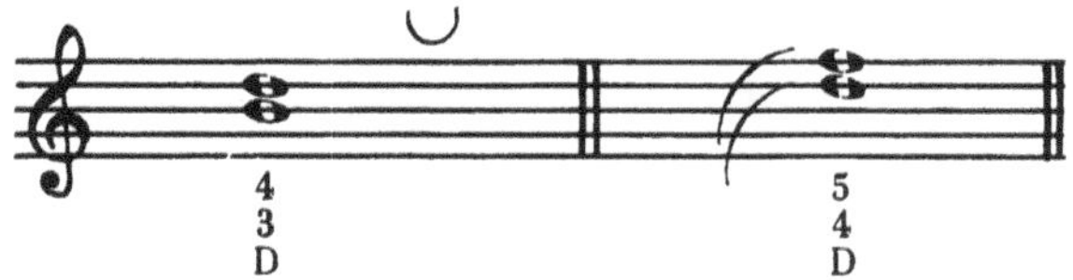

Play these.

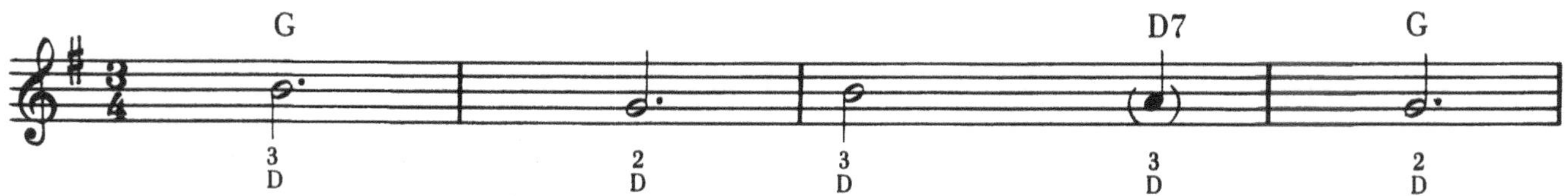

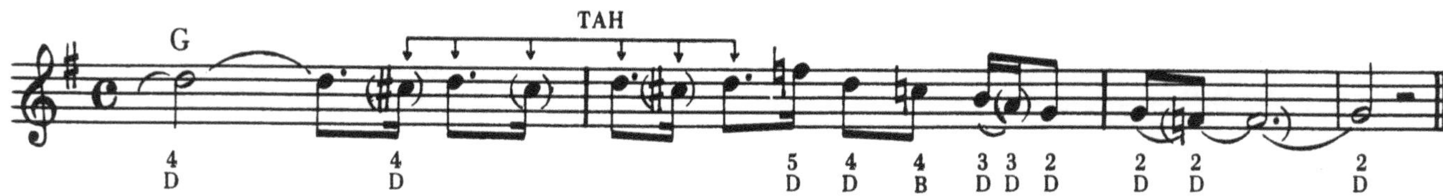

Some Special Effects

There are a number of special effects that are widely used. Study and practice these, as they are basic and will give you a good foundation upon which to later build and create effects of your own.

THE GLISS (SHORT FOR GLISSANDO) OR RIP. Just before playing a note, rapidly slide the harmonica across the lips 2, 3 or 4 holes above or below the note to be played. The notes are sounded very quickly and not as loud as the note you land on. Effective blow and draw. Indicated by a wavy line up to or down to the note (⁓ ⁓).

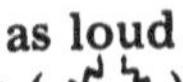

THE TRAIN WHISTLE. Alternately open and close the hands (move the Right Hand only, like a slow vibrato). This produces a WAH-WAH. At the same time play two notes together. With the hands open, play at pitch. As you close the hands, bend the notes down. As you open the hands again, let the notes come back up to pitch.

THE TRAIN. The warhorse of harmonica tricks.

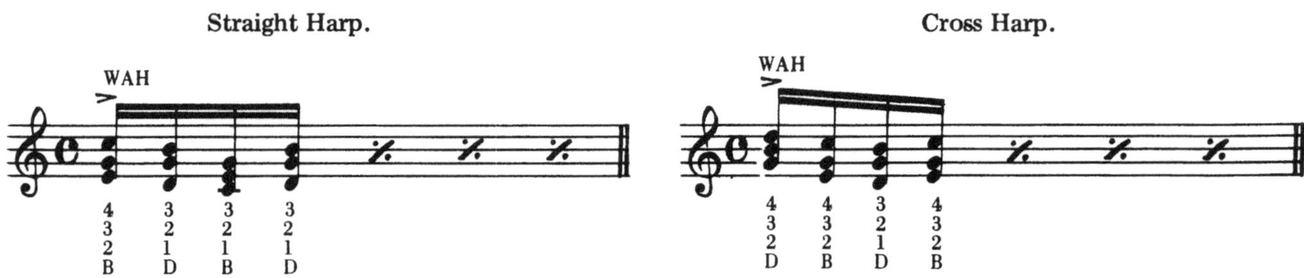

The first chord of each group of four has an accent (>). Play this chord a little louder, at the same time opening the hands — WAH. Close the hands for the next three chords. Vary the tempo — start slow and speed up, then slow down. Add the train whistle.

TREMOLO. There are two kinds. The first is the rapid reiteration of a note. This is done by Lipping a note and very rapidly moving the tongue from side to side while it is pressed against the lips. This causes the air column to start and stop. Effective for one or more notes, both blow and draw. The second kind, and most often used, is the rapid alternation of two notes. Hold the harmonica in the Right Hand, and shake it rapidly back and forth so that you alternately play two different holes. You will generally start a tremolo with the higher note (D to F, play the F first). Good for blow and draw.

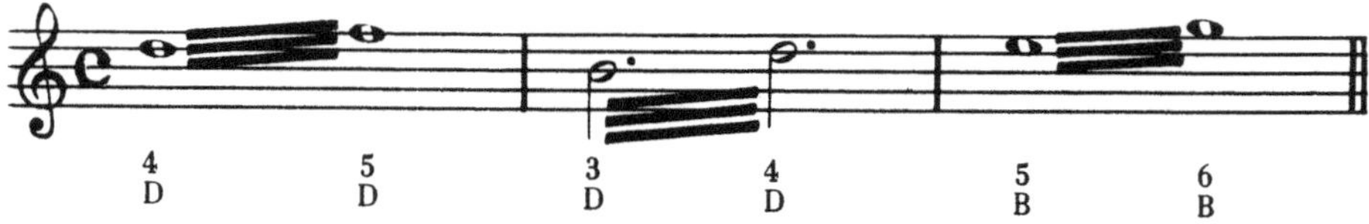

Vary the speed from slow to fast. This is how it is generally played. As you tremolo, bend the notes down, then let back up to pitch. You've probably heard this or something close to it.

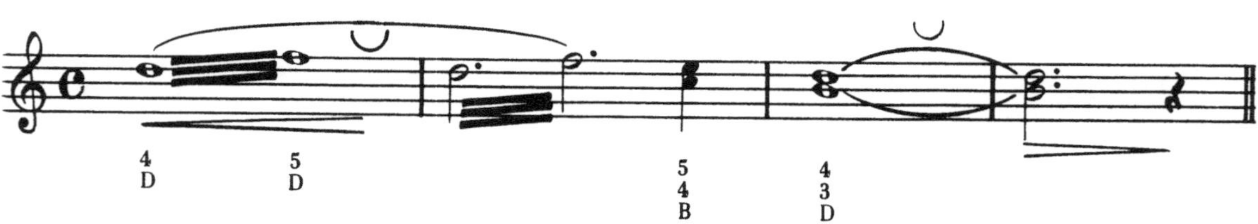

TALKING EFFECTS. While blowing or drawing two or more notes, try forming words with your mouth. Say "Hello There". Notice how the sound or timbre of the tone changes? Try "Feeling Low". "Goodby". Experiment with other word sounds and see what they do to the quality of the tone.

TONGUED RHYTHM. This is the basis for all accompaniment rhythms. Sharp, smart, intricate chord patterns are playable.

Try the following:

THIN SOUND	FULL SOUND	ATTACK	CUT-OFF
Say HIT		soft	sharp
" HIH		soft	soft
" IT		med. soft	sharp
" TIT		sharp	sharp
	Say HOT	soft	sharp
	" HAH	soft	soft
	" OUGHT	med. soft	sharp
	" TOT	sharp	sharp

Try some other word sounds. Find those that are most comfortable for you to use. Much of the time I use TUT or DUT as the basic syllable.

Some rhythmic type accompaniments.

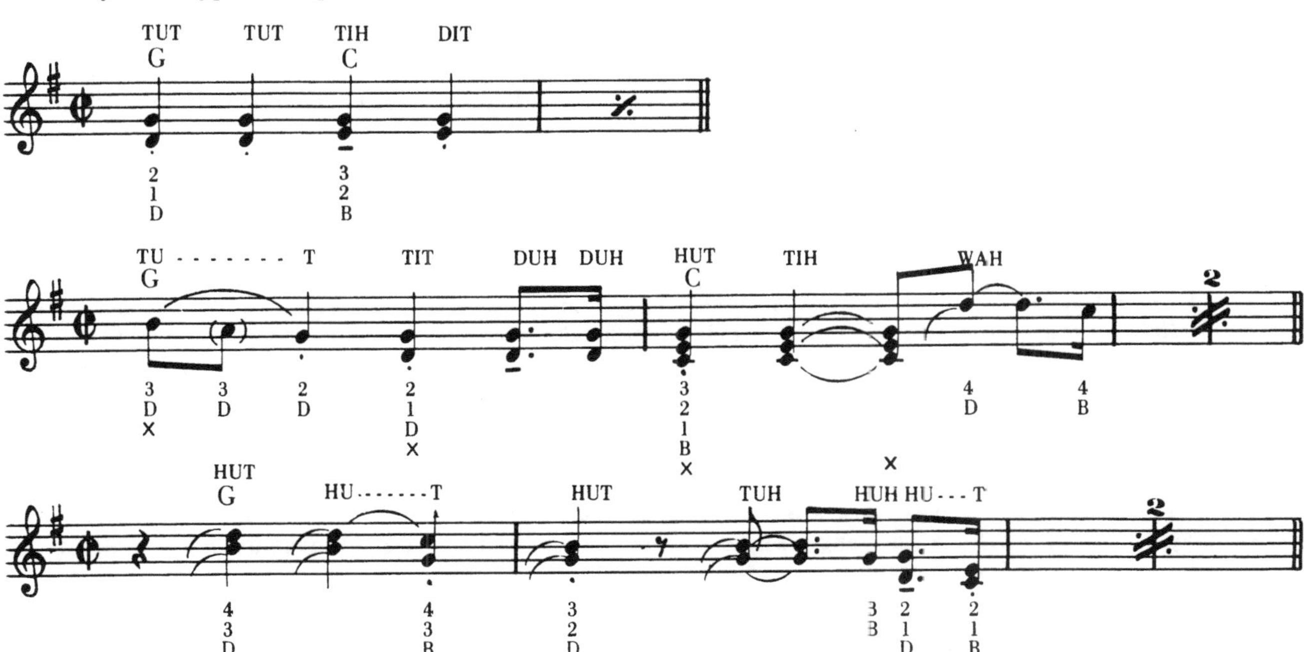

SINGLE TONGUE. To play a short sharp note or chord. Say TUT or DUT.

DOUBLE TONGUE. To play repeated notes or chords in groups of two. Say DIDDLE-DIDDLE-DIDDLE or TUKA-TUKA-TUKA. DIDDLE is a softer effect while TUKA is much sharper.

TRIPLE TONGUE. To play repeated notes or chords in groups of three. Say DIDDLE-LA-DIDDLE-LA-DIDDLE-LA or TUKA-TA-TUKA-TA-TUKA-TA. DIDDLE-LA is a softer effect while TUKA-TA is much sharper.

THE GROWL. Produced by rolling the R sound on the tongue for blow notes. Draw notes are difficult. These are played either by inhaling and using the tongue something like the blow growl, or by drawing and making a sound like snoring (and then remove the "sound"). Either way is difficult, and hard to make sound like the blow. However, once mastered, it can be effectively used for both single notes and chords.

Use these effects sparingly. Don't do them just because you can play them. Wait for the right time, when they really fit the music and become a part of it, rather than just some sound to be used for its own sake.

Chapter Three

Creating Your Own Fills and Solos

To be able to play with other musicians offers the greatest challenge to the player. What do I play? When do I play? These are the questions to be answered.

The good musician realizes that playing with other musicians doesn't mean for each man to go his own way and create his own "thing". He listens to what is going on around him and bases what he does on what the others are doing.

The harmonica part for one of the music cues from the motion picture "Cable Hogue" looked something like this:

When to play was easy, since the composer knew exactly where he wanted the "funky" harmonica sound. What to play, was the question. After listening to the cue, it became evident what type of rhythm to play, and what type of solo could be heard with the orchestra playing.

I used Cross Harp to get the funky sound, the Wail to be heard above the orchestra, and waited for openings to play low choked rhythms. This proved to be a very effective cue.

The important thing to do is to LISTEN. Buy the records of the groups you like that feature harmonica (Cream, Paul Butterfield, Canned Heat, Them, etc.). The greatest figure or fill will be thrown out if it doesn't fit with what the rest of the group is doing. Maybe they'll take what you're doing, and build on it. Great. But when you've finally put it all together, everything has to fit, and what doesn't sound right should be discarded.

WHAT TO LISTEN FOR. The bass player plays a good line for 8 bars using a repeating figure. Maybe you can play the lick with him as part of the rhythm section, or use part of it for your own solo. You played a great intro, fill with something from the intro music, either the same or slightly changed. Use something from the song or something the singer used that was slightly different than the original tune. Echo the singer's last few notes (play a little of what she just sang). You create your own "melody", and maybe use a rhythm that you heard the drummer or guitar player use.

Guitar plays:

After 2 bars bass joins in; 2 bars later you play:

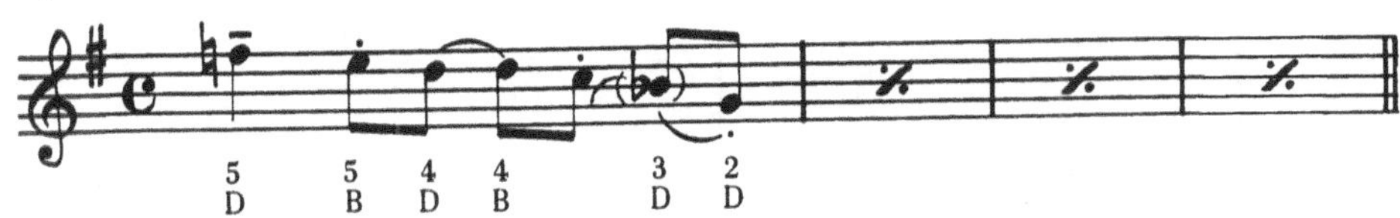

A Solo

Original melody using rhythmic pattern from guitar and drums.

4 D 5 D | 5 4 B | 4 3 D 2 D | 2 D

Rhythm Section G × × × × | × × × ×

WAH 6 D | 6 B 5 D 5 B 4 B | WAH 4 D | 3 D 4 B

C | | G |

4 D 5 D | 4 D | 4 B | 2 D 2 D

D7 | | C |

Vibrato 2 D | | |

G | | |

Solo Variations

Solo 1 portrays the melody as written.

Solo 2 contains more notes and rhythmic variations.

Solo 3 is a more advanced version of Solo 2 with even more notes and more advanced rhythmic variations.

Harmonica background accompaniment for guitar or other instrumental solo.

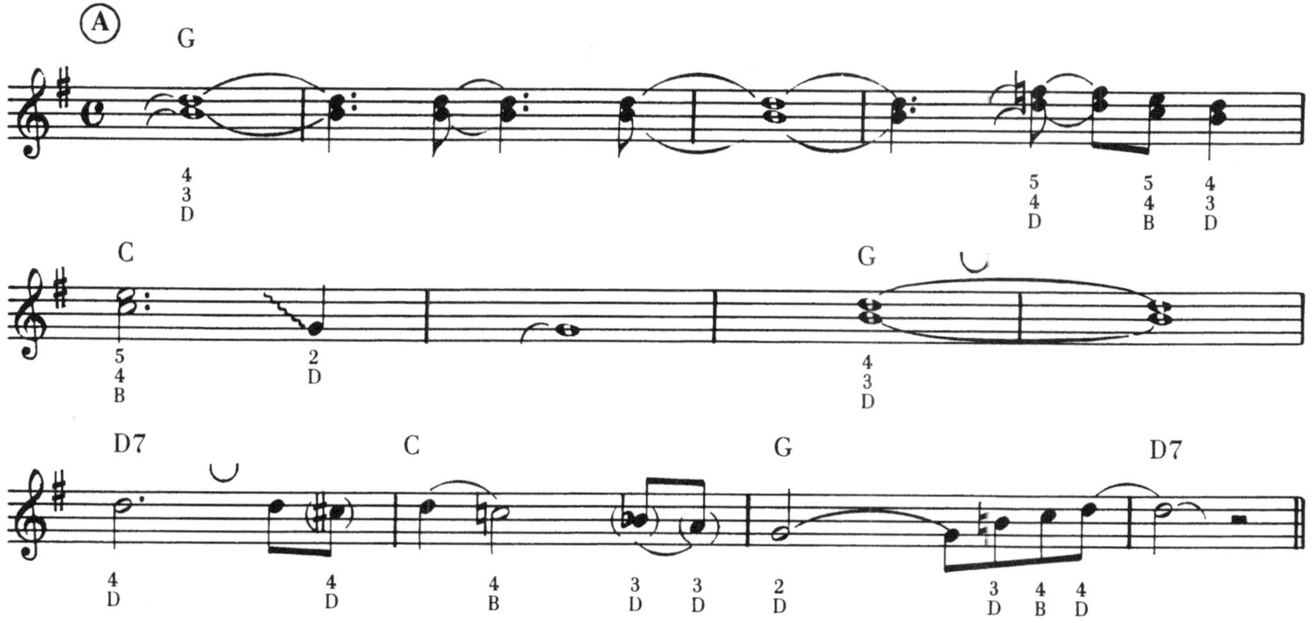

Letter A is a standard background. Letter B is the last chorus. Notice that the part is busier.

These examples at best are only guidelines to open the door to creative blues playing. Your ear is still the best teacher for style. The purpose of this section has been to give you a basic understanding of how some of the things are done. Listen to records. This will show you what has been done in the past, and what is being done today. The reason for practicing the basic skills is to let you control the instrument so that when you "hear" something in your mind, your technique will allow you to play it.

I Want You, My Baby

Words and Music by
TOMMY MORGAN
A.S.C.A.P.

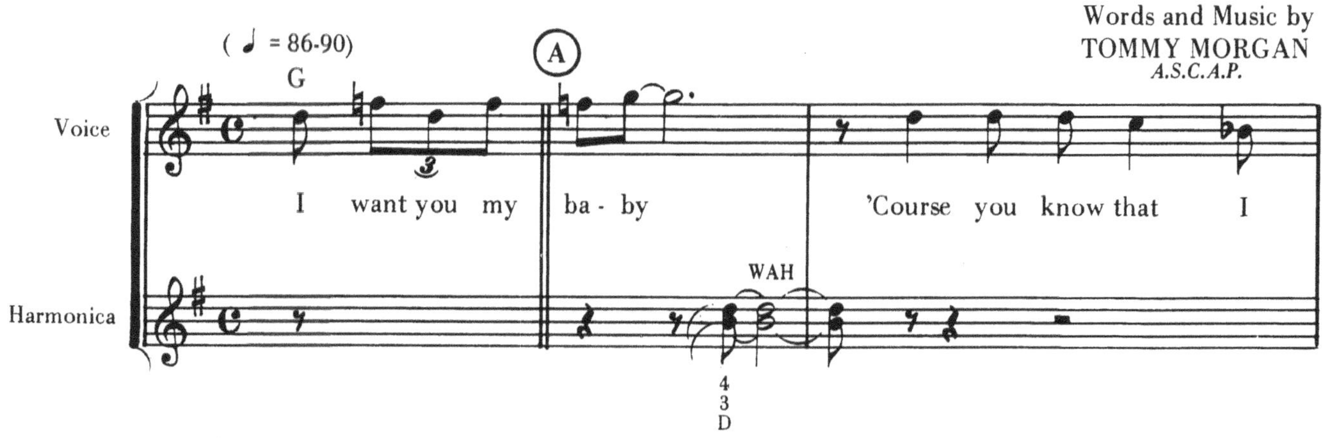

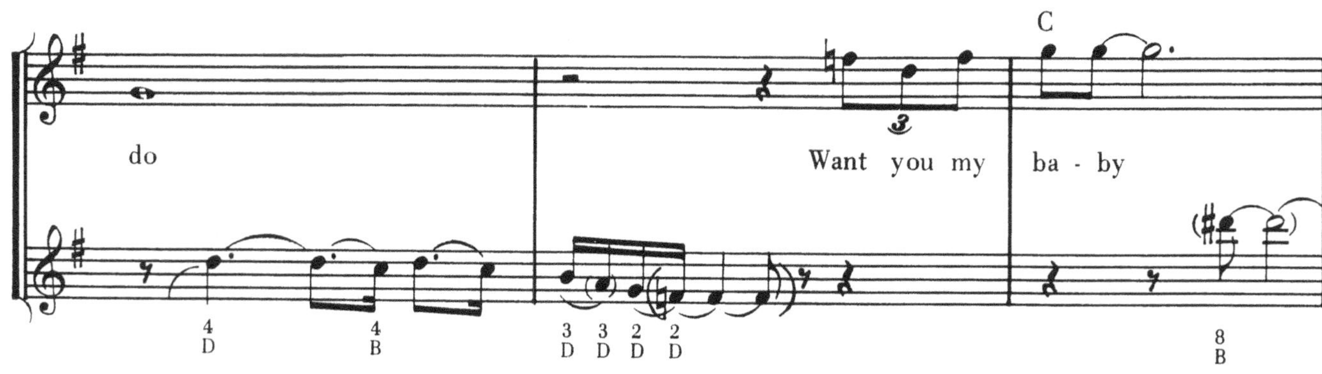

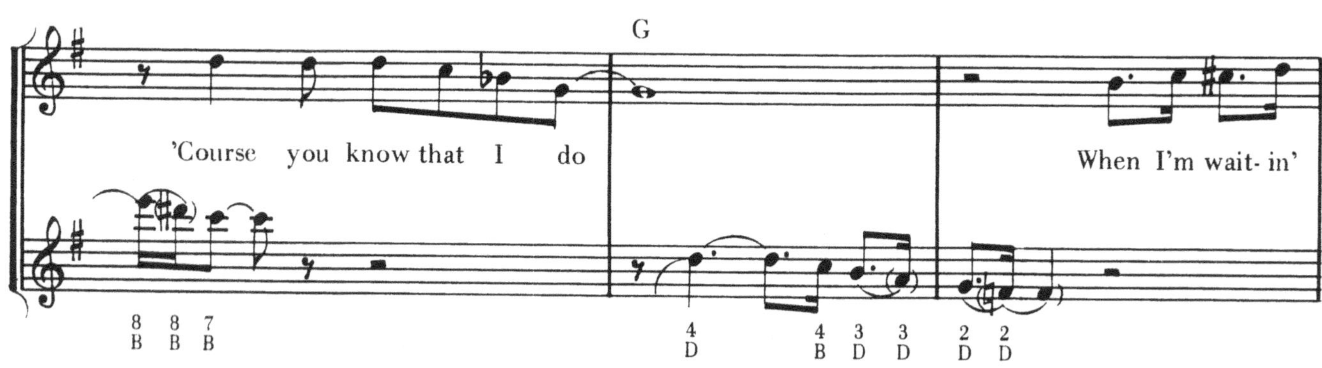

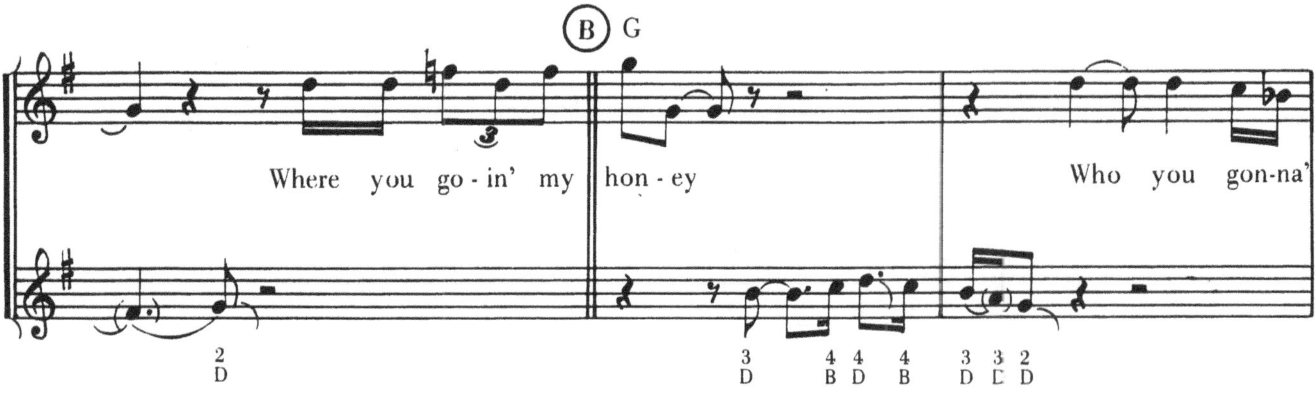
B
G
Where you go - in' my hon - ey
Who you gon-na'

C
see
Where to my hon - ey

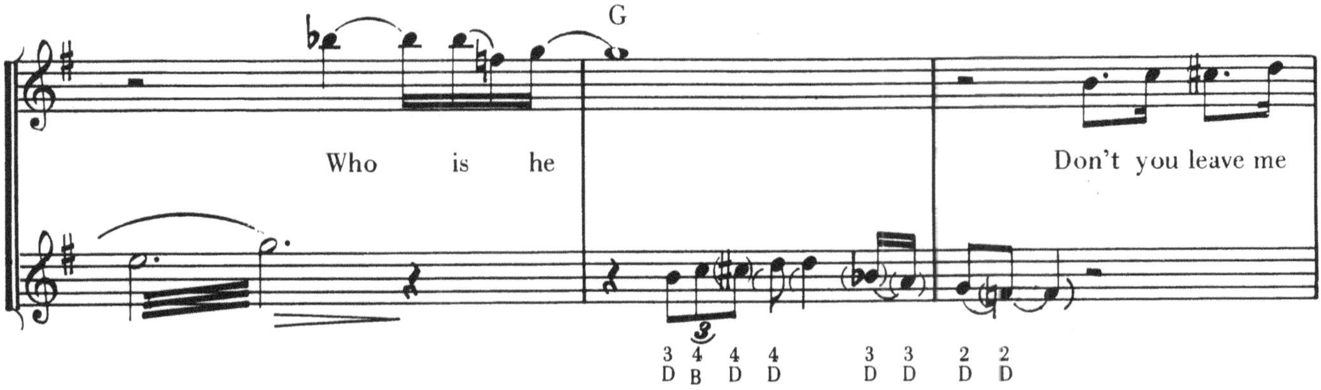
G
Who is he
Don't you leave me

D7
C
G
ba - by
Wan - na' know where you be.
WAH
*Bend G down to F♮

Chapter Four

How To Play In Other Keys

Since the Diatonic Harmonica is made in all 12 keys, we can play in any key simply by using the correct harmonica for the new key. This is true for both Straight Harp and Cross Harp.

When you play C on a C Harmonica — it sounds C

When you play C on a D Harmonica — it sounds D

When you play C on a B♭ Harmonica — it sounds B♭

If you want to play this melody in the key of C, on a C Harmonica you play

If you want to play this same melody in the key of D, on a D Harmonica you play (like on the C Harmonica)

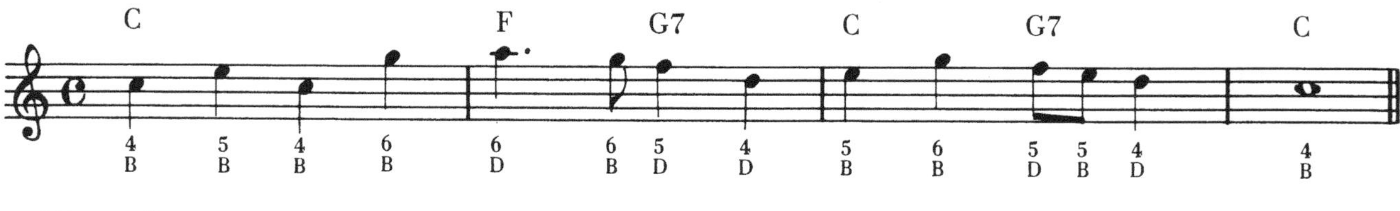

and it sounds

All of the harmonicas and keys work this way. Play as if you were in the key of C, and whatever harmonica you use (E♭ , G, B♭ , etc.) that is the key you will be playing in.

Look back to Page 10 and play the example. With an A Harmonica, it sounds in the key of A.

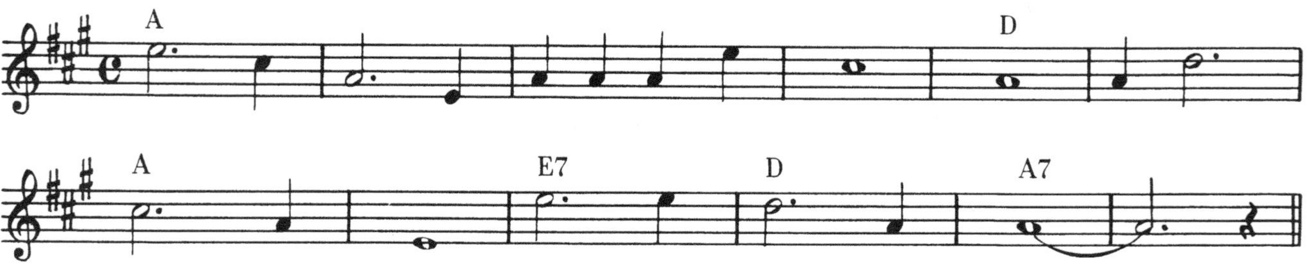

For Cross Harp, we have to be aware of the dominant chords for the different harmonicas. For the D Harmonica, draw holes #1 — #4, and you get the dominant, which is A. To play in the Key of A using Cross Harp First Position, we need a D Harmonica. To play in the Key of F, we need the harmonica whose dominant is F — that's a B♭ Harmonica. For a complete list of all Cross Harp Positions and Keys, see Appendix A. This will show you which harmonica to use to play in each key.

As you have now discovered, harmonicas in different keys sound different. This is because they are higher or lower than the C Harmonica. The G Harmonica is the lowest sounding instrument.

The harmonicas in each of the succeeding keys (G♯ A B♭ B C C♯ D E♭ E F F♯) are built ½ step higher than the other. The highest sounding harmonica is F.

While you play the harmonicas the same way, each one will have its own feel because it sounds higher or lower than the others, and certain notes will bend easier on one harmonica than another. You will find yourself adapting to this without really thinking about it. The lower harmonicas are great for choked rhythms and mid-range Cross Harp solos. The upper octave is good for some Wailing. The higher sounding harmonicas are fine for piercing Cross Harp solos, but the upper octave really is too high for much Wailing, and the lower octave too high for good choked rhythms. Good keys for higher Cross Harp First Position solos are A through C (Harmonicas D—F). Good keys for darker lower choked rhythms (or long low double stops for the softer tunes) are D through F (Harmonicas G—B♭). These are generalizations. Special or different chord changes can make a big difference.

If you have to play a piercing Cross Harp solo in the key of D (G Harmonica — the lowest sounding of all), and you want lots of mid and upper range draw notes, you may have to go to another Cross Harp Position.

Chapter Five

Advanced Cross Harp Positions

There are two other Cross Harp Positions, not as widely used, but important to know and understand.

CROSS HARP — SECOND POSITION. The harmonica is one whole step below the key. Key of D/C Harmonica. The chord and non-chord tones that may be played.

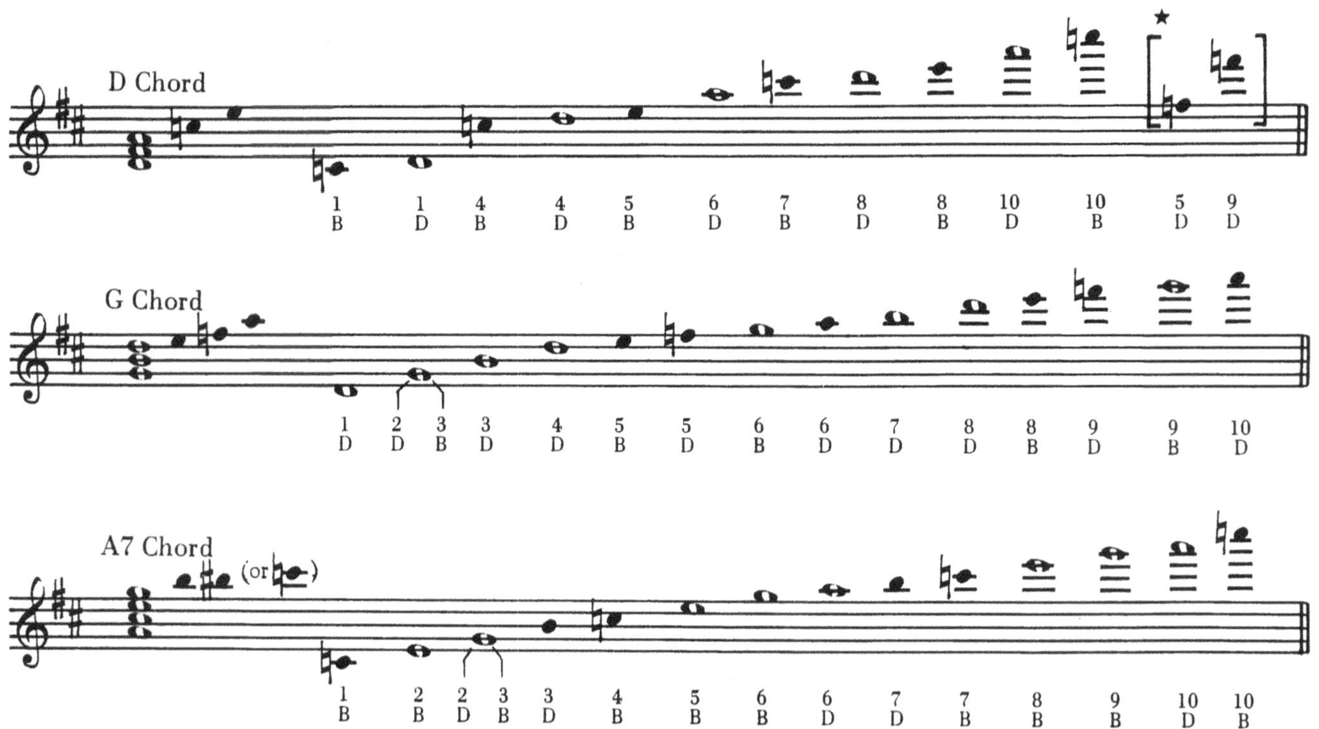

Some fills and figures.

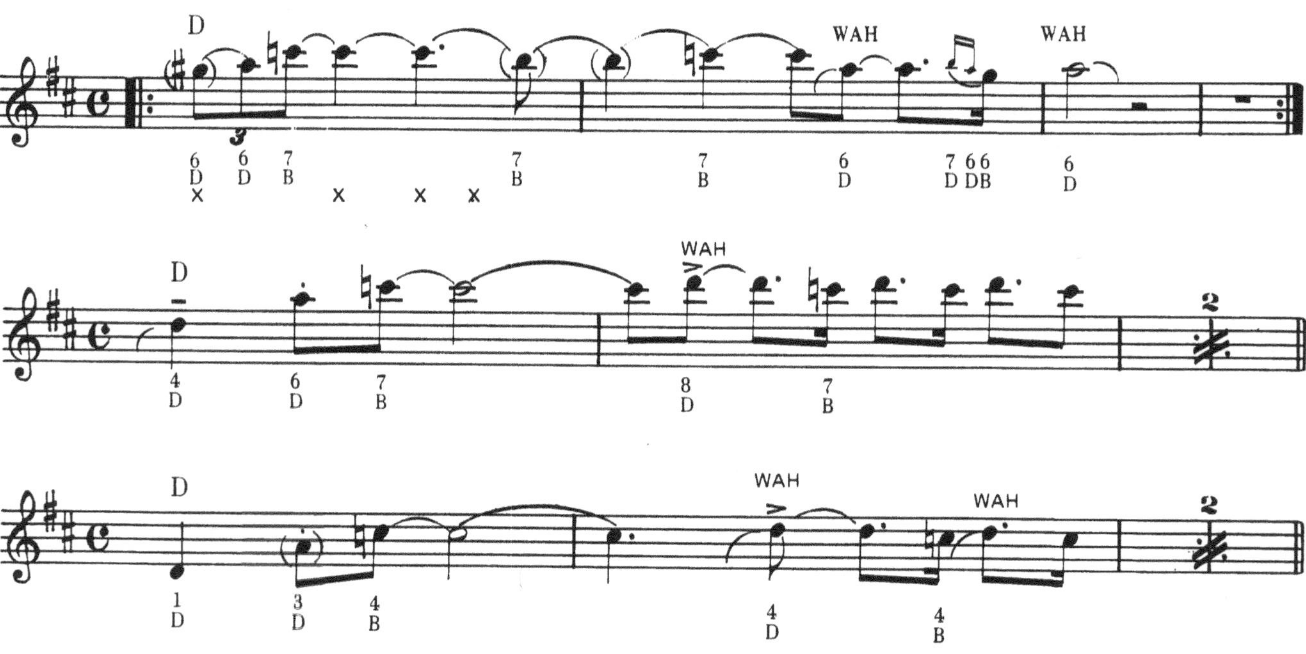

* May also be used.

Solo in D Major.

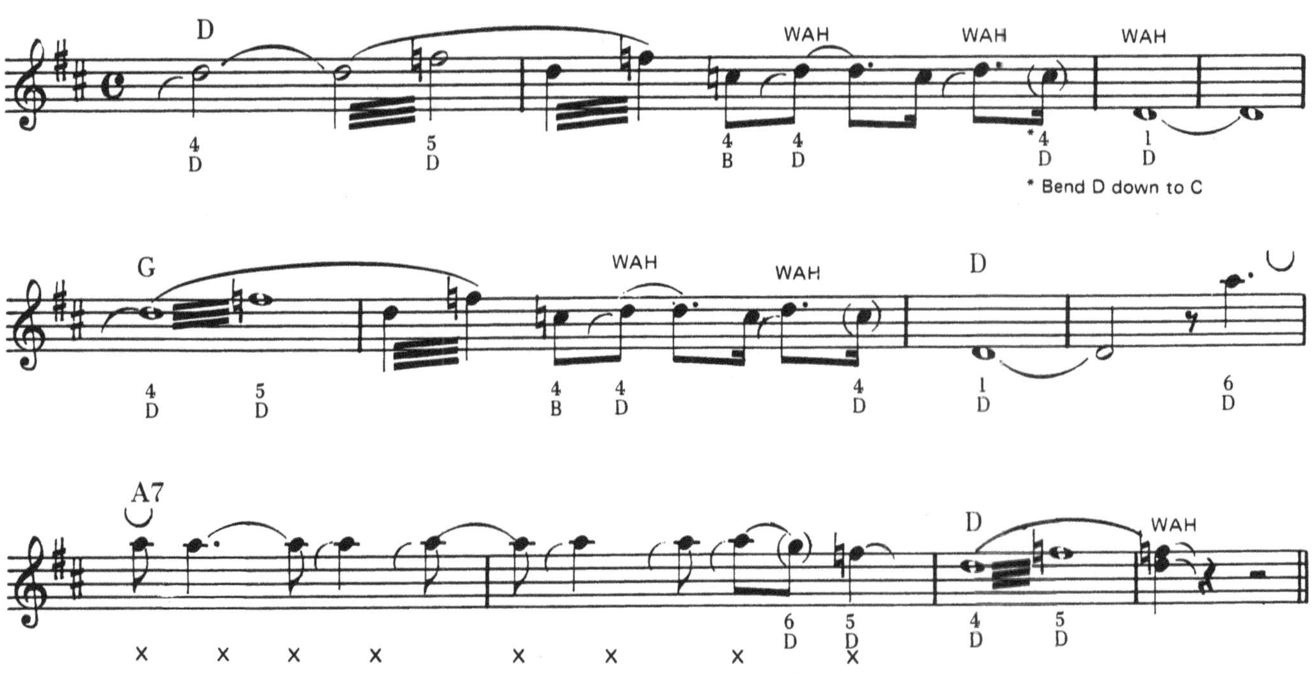

CROSS HARP — THIRD POSITION. The harmonica is a major third below the key. Key of E/C Harmonica.

The chord and non-chord tones that may be played.

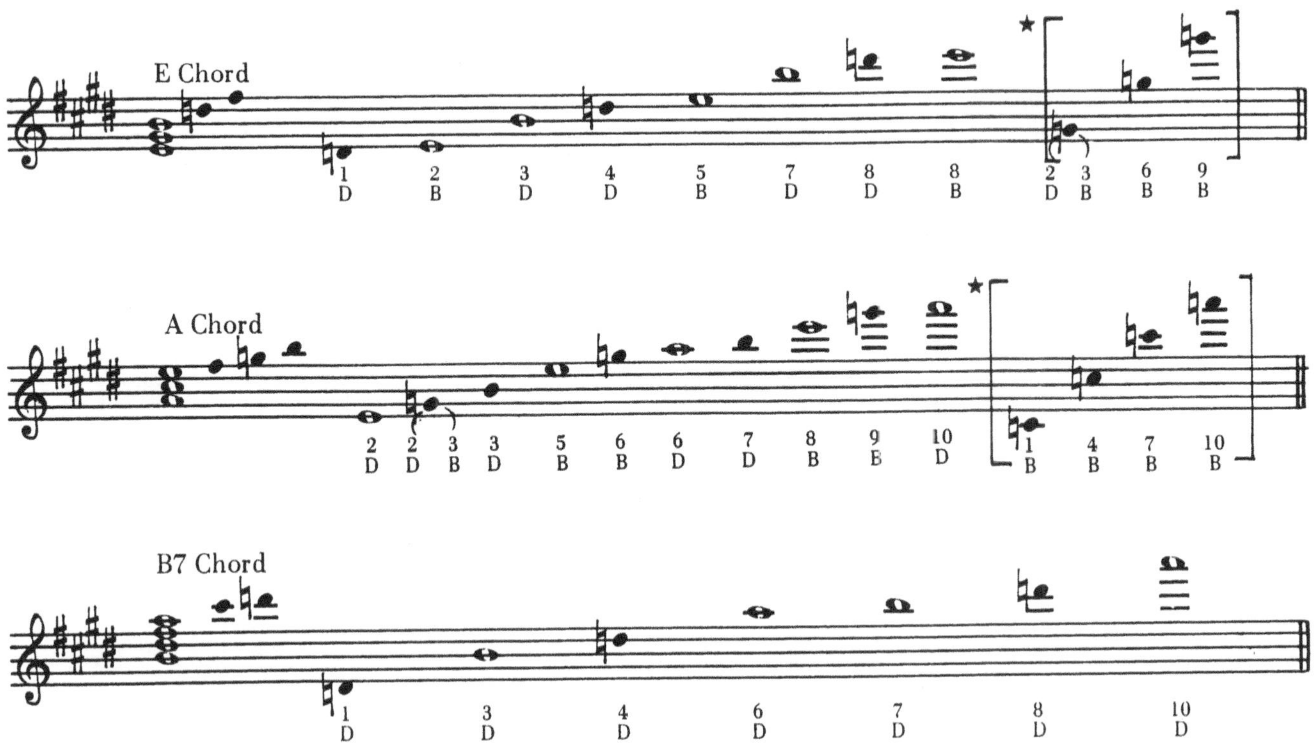

★ May also be used.

Some fills and figures.

Solo in E Major.

For a complete list of all Cross Harp Positions for each key, see Appendix A.

Don't let this section confuse you. Stay with First Position until you feel that you really understand it. Then do a little work with the advanced positions. Don't rush into them. Remember, most of your playing will be in First Position.

Chapter Six

Playing In Minor Keys

Until recently, relatively little playing had been done in minor keys. The harmonica players were unfamiliar with the Straight and Cross Harp Positions that fit the minor chords.

This section will serve as an introduction to playing in minor keys. By now you should have a good idea of what to do after studying the examples showing the chord and non-chord tones that may be played on the harmonica for each chord.

To hear a minor chord, draw holes #4—#6. This is a D Minor chord. Minor music is usually darker sounding music. In general you bend the notes slower, giving more of a moaning style to your playing.

The three basic chords in C Minor are:

G7 chord — Dominant Seventh. The same for C Major and C Minor

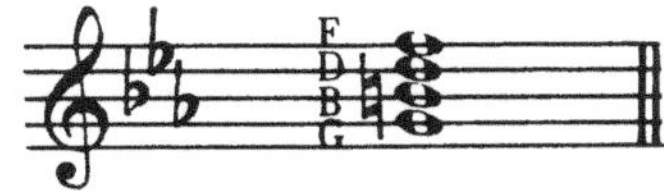

Straight Harp

Key of C Minor/C Harmonica. The chord and non-chord tones that may be played.

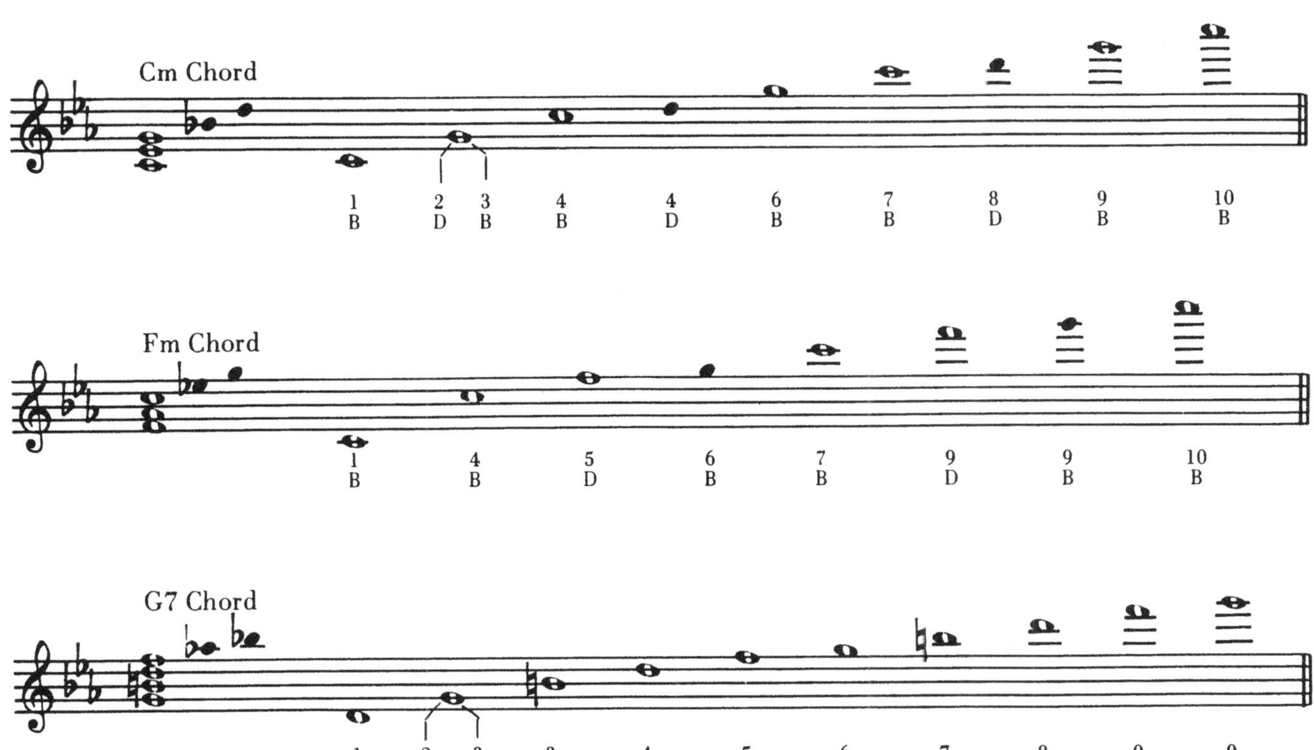

Solo in C Minor. Think of those notes that you can bend down to fit the chords.

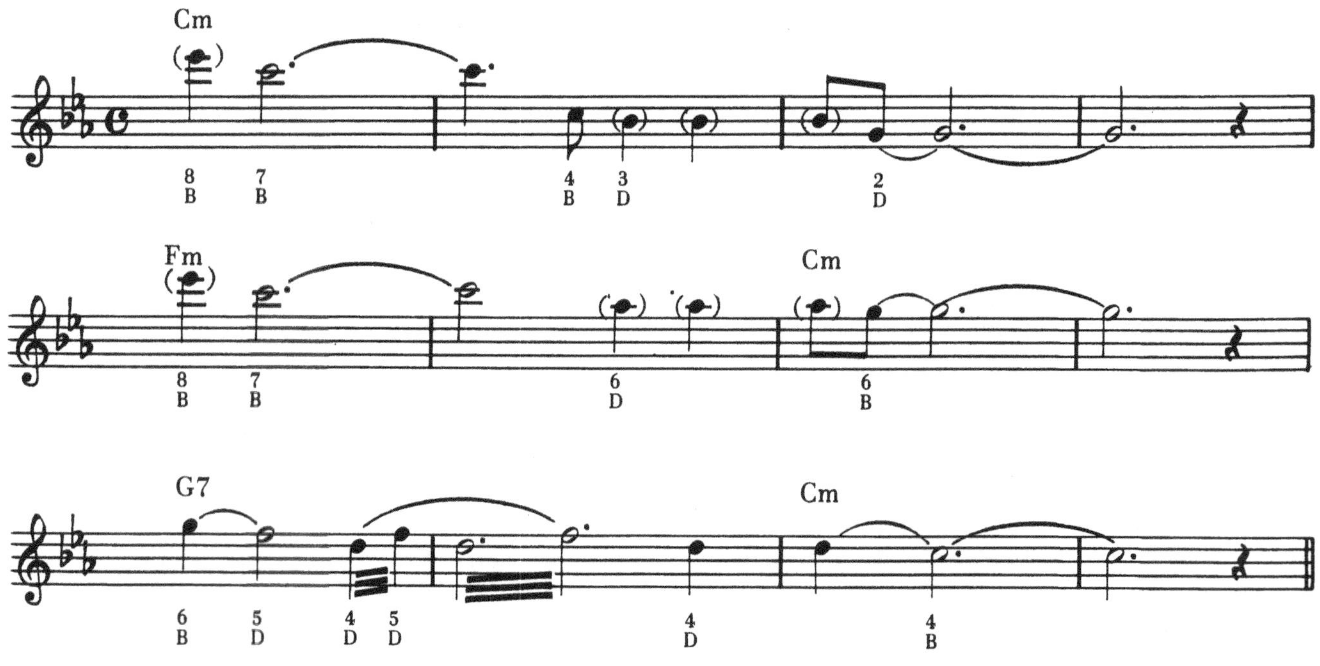

Cross Harp

The three most important ways of playing in minor keys are Cross Harp First, Second and Third Positions.

CROSS HARP — FIRST POSITION. The harmonica is a minor 3rd above the key. Key of A Minor/C Harmonica. The chord and non-chord tones that may be played.

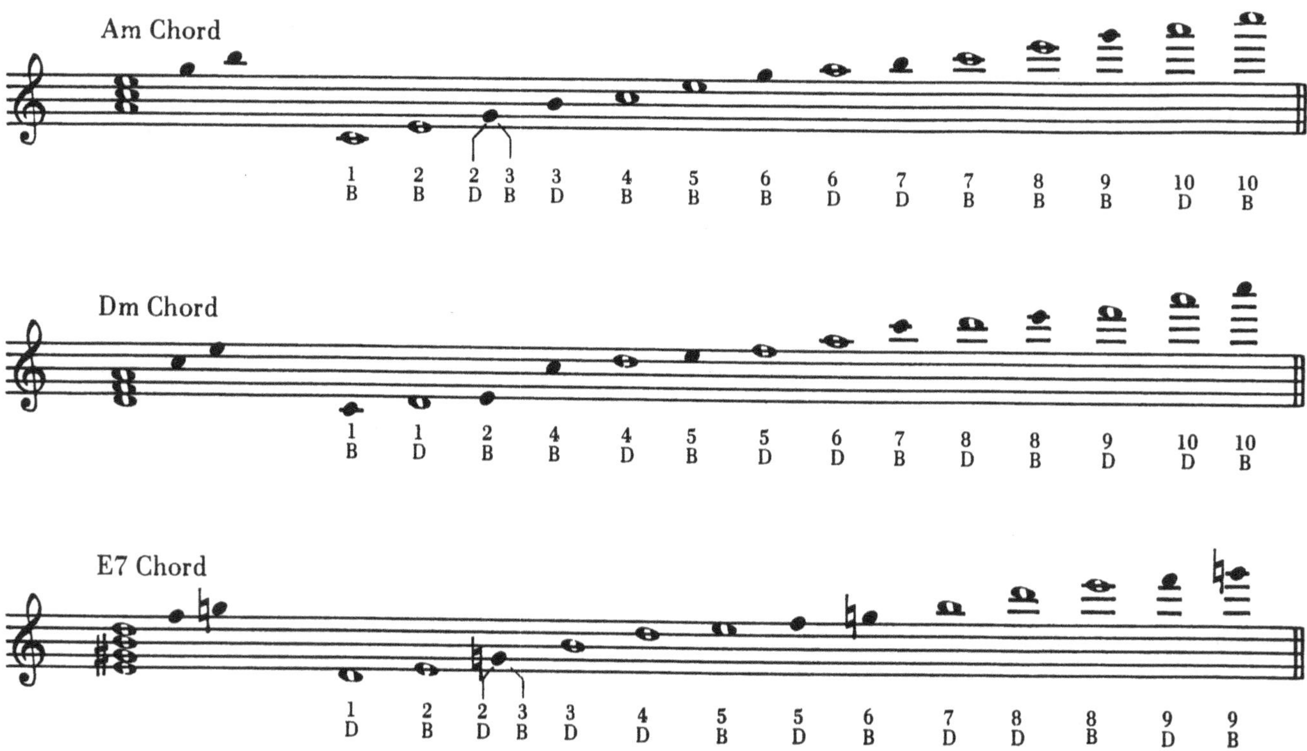

Solo in A Minor.

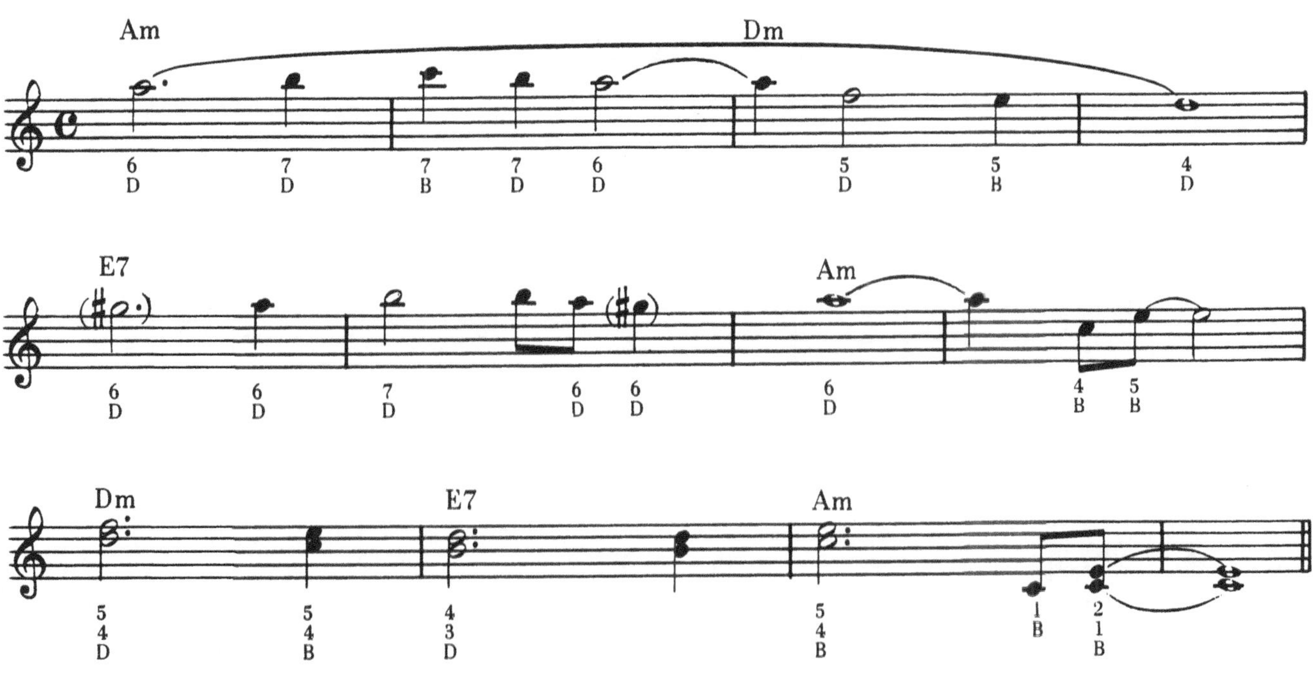

CROSS HARP – SECOND POSITION. The harmonica is one whole step below the key. Key of D Minor/C Harmonica. The chord and non-chord tones that may be played.

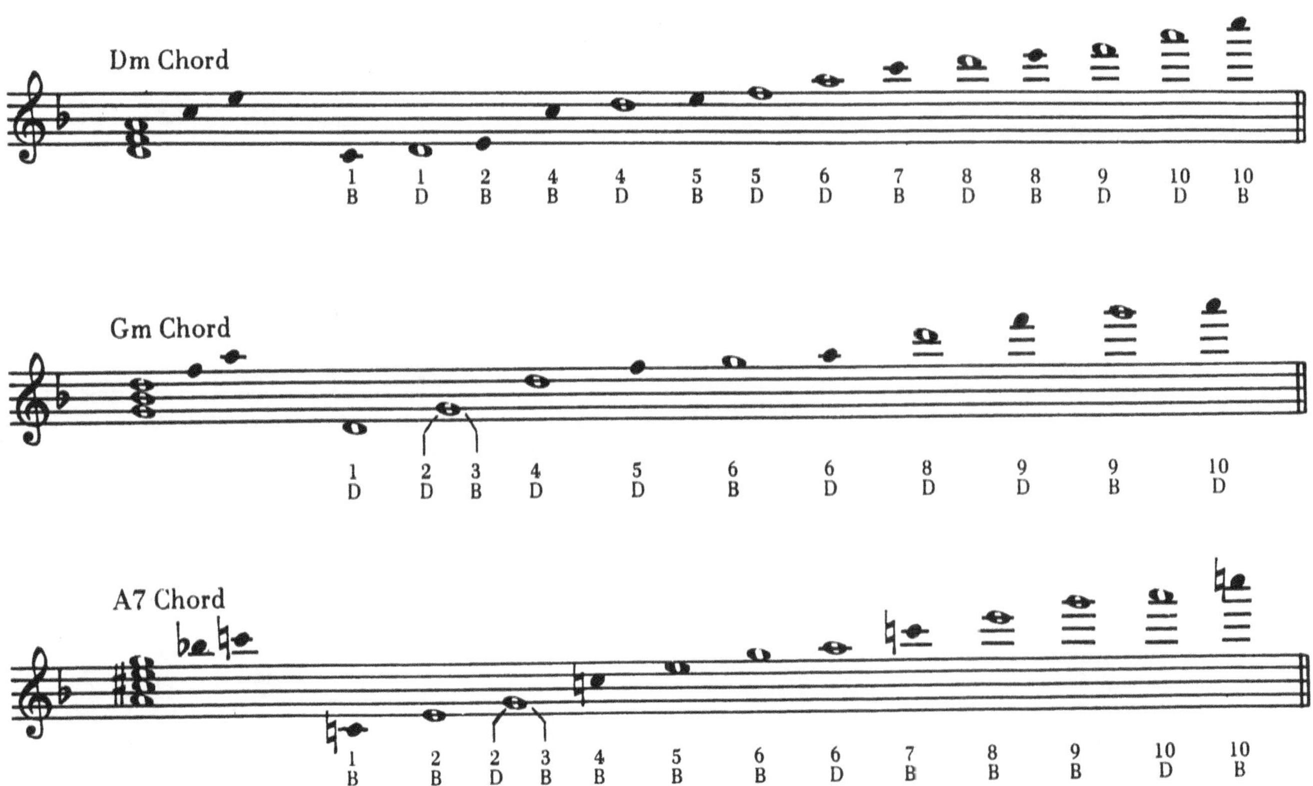

Solo in D Minor.

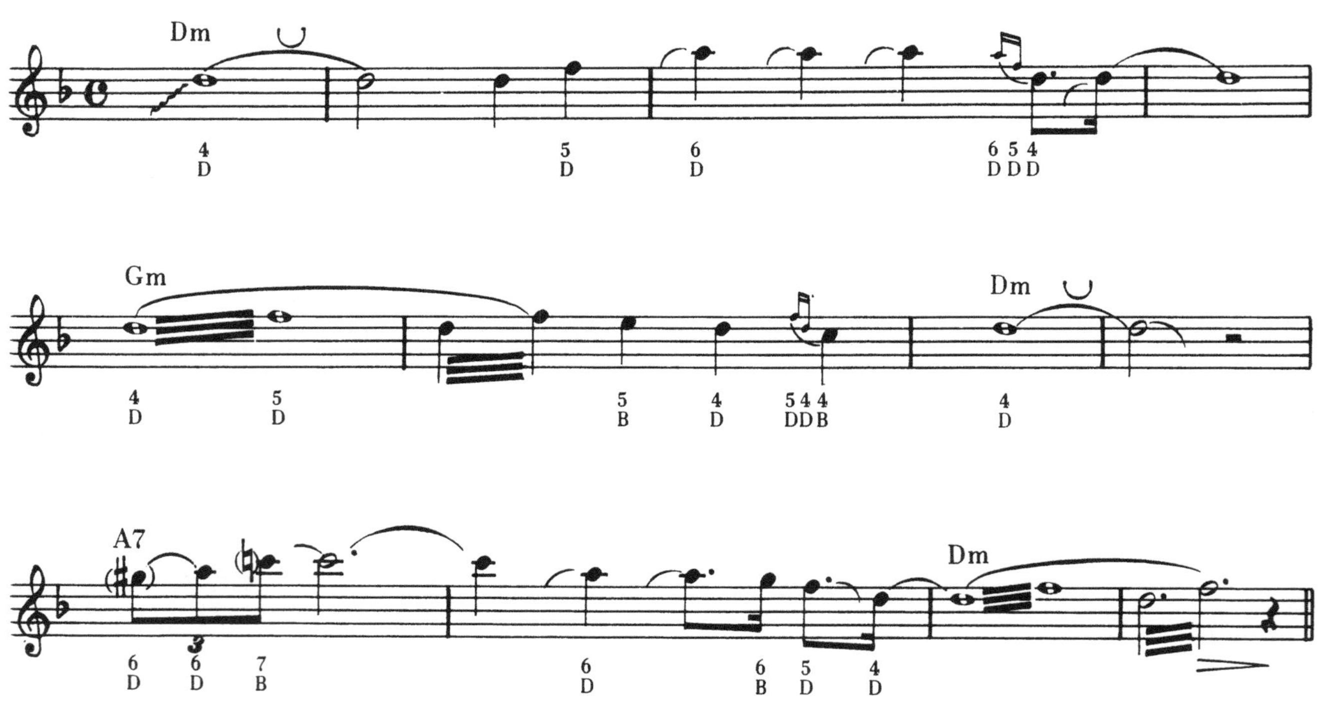

CROSS HARP — THIRD POSITION. The harmonica is a major 3rd below the key. Key of E Minor/C Harmonica. The chord and non-chord tones that may be played.

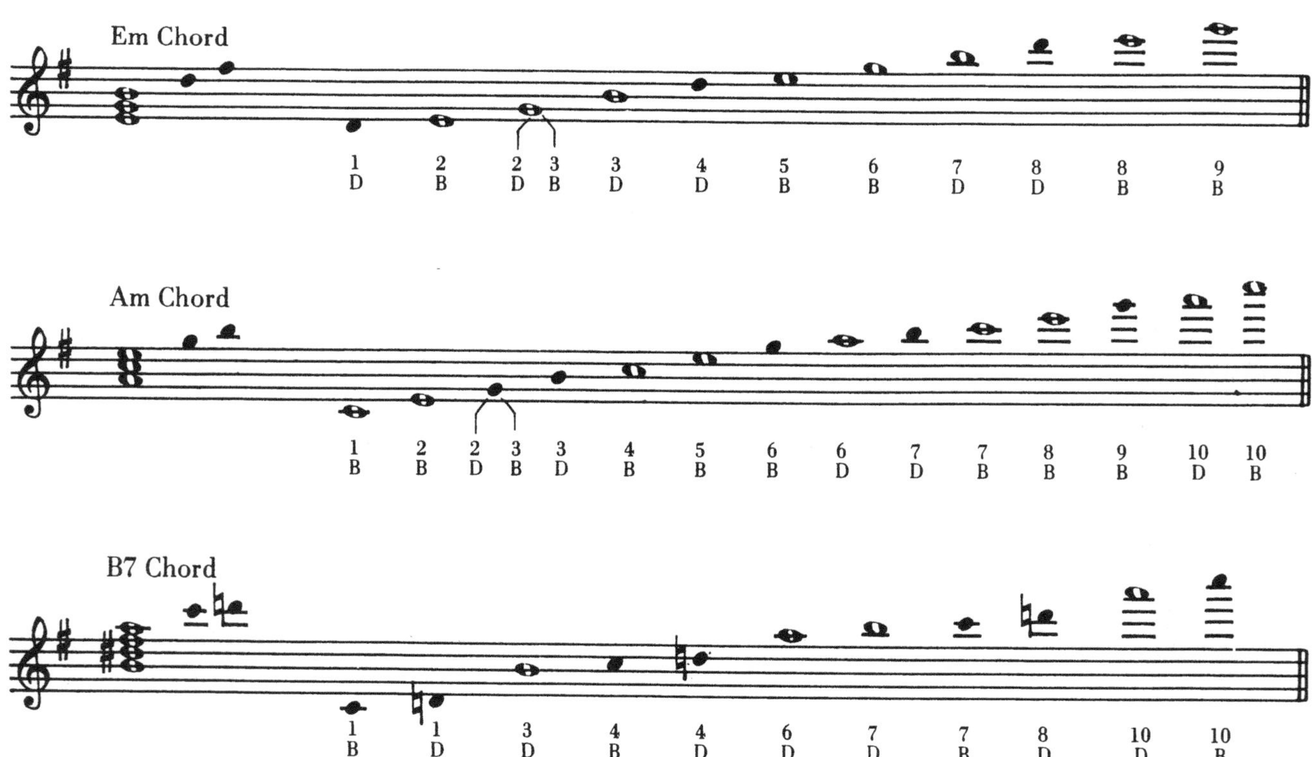

Solo in E Minor.

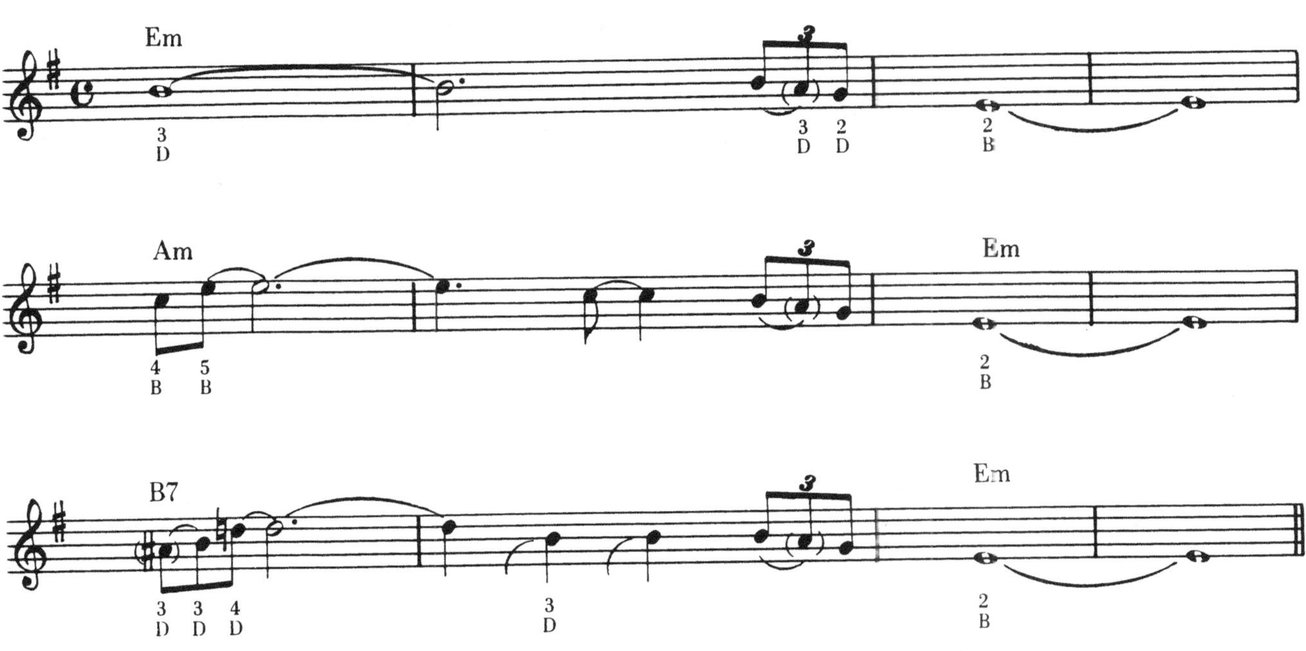

CROSS HARP — FOURTH POSITION. The harmonica is ½ step above the key. Key of B Minor/C Harmonica. The chord and non-chord tones that may be played.

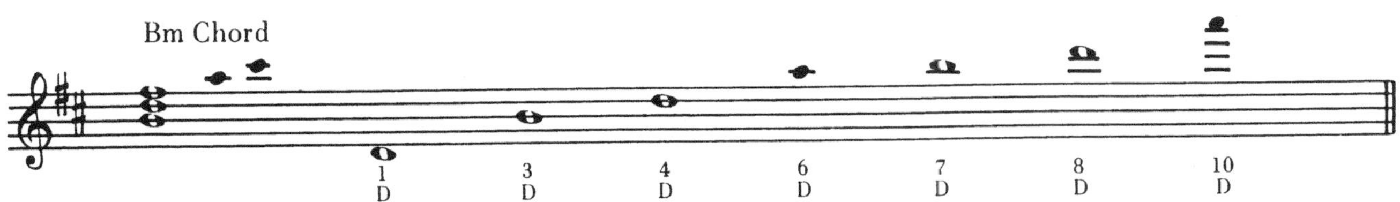

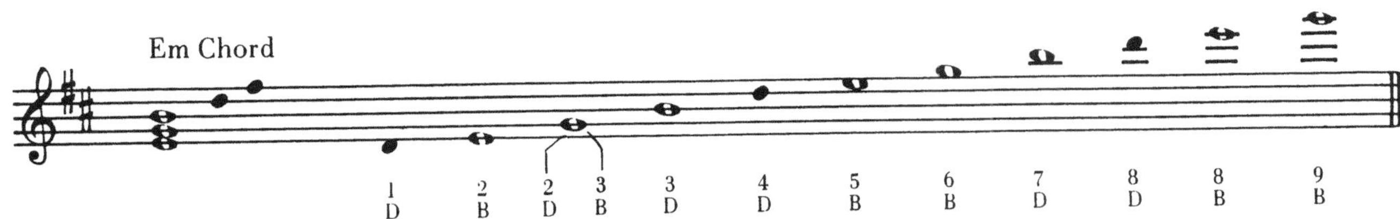

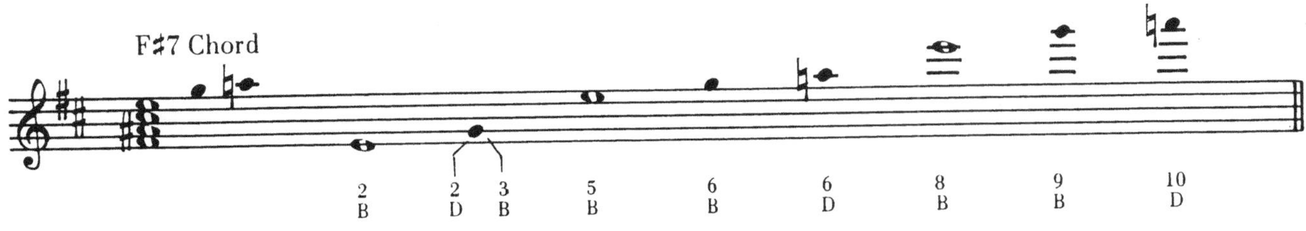

Solo in B Minor.

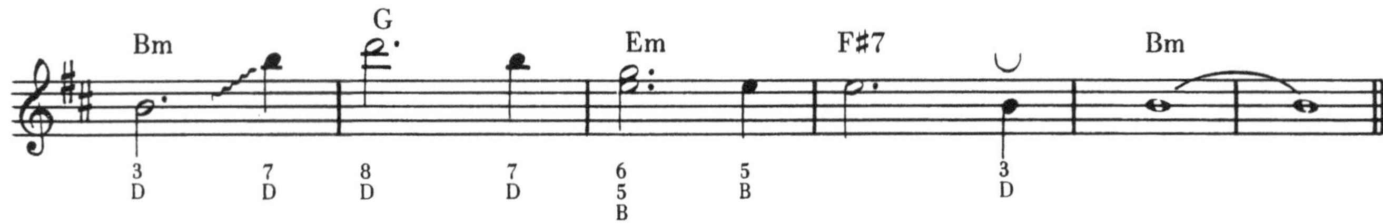

For a complete list of all Cross Harp Positions for each key, see Appendix A.

Chapter Seven

Using More Than One Harmonica

There are times when more than one harmonica should be used. Any number of reasons exist. You can hold two harmonicas in your hands at the same time, and go back and forth between them. If you do it smoothly enough, no one will know that you are switching. You can even use hand vibrato.

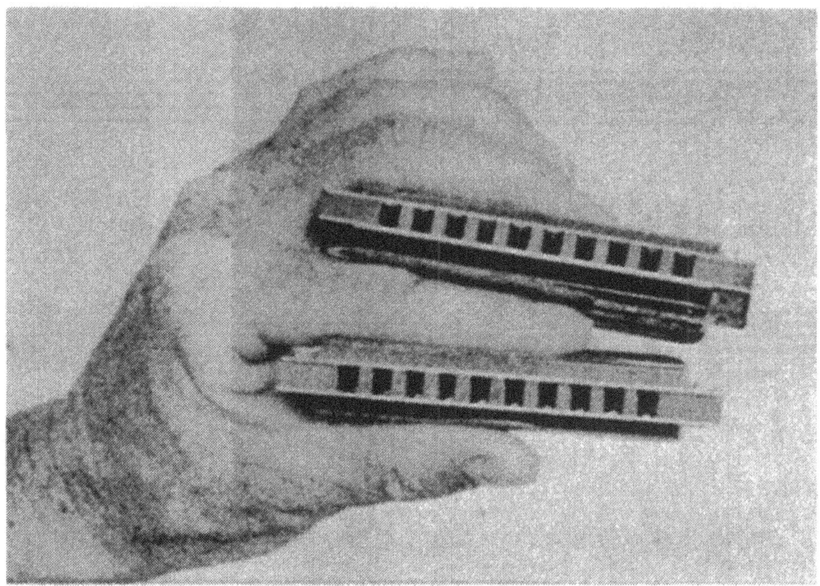

You can also use tremolo. Separate the hands, keeping the harmonica you want to shake for tremolo in your Right Hand, the other in your Left. When finished, bring the hands together again.

The real trick here is to remember which harmonica to play at which time when you're switching back and forth. To be consistent, I generally hold the instrument where I play the tonic on the bottom.

Before going any farther, be sure you understand Cross Harp completely. As already stated, most of your playing will be Cross Harp First Position. When you come across something you can't play that way, then go to the advanced Cross Harp positions and/or more than one harmonica. It's complex, but this is how it is done.

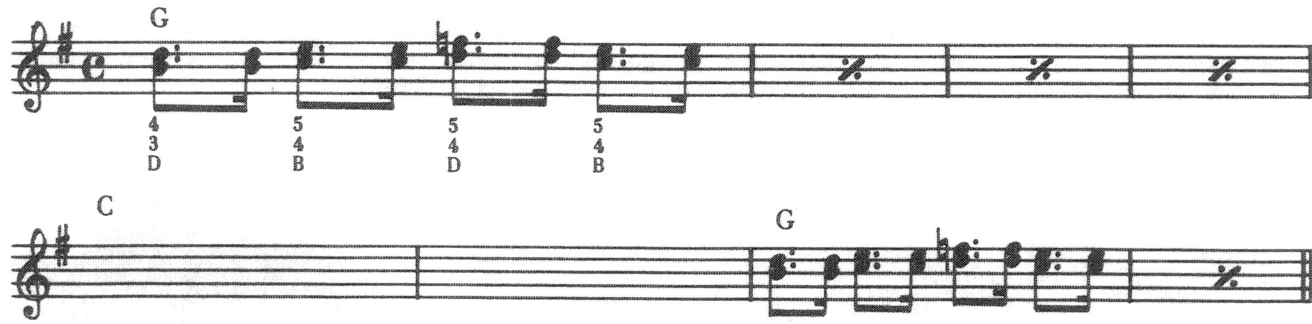

To play the same pattern for the C chord, take an F harmonica and play as you did in bar 1, above.

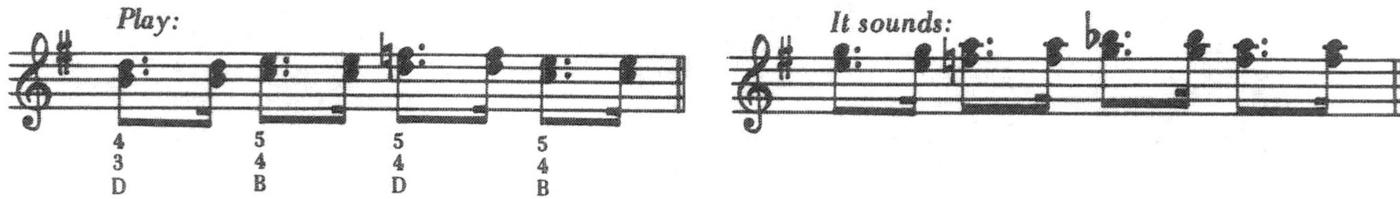

I have only briefly described what to do. The more you play, the more you will discover. The combinations are endless, and far too numerous to describe.

You can hold up to 4 harmonicas at one time, but this is rarely done. It becomes cumbersome and hard to handle. The only occasion when I've found it necessary to use 4, was for the motion picture, "The Reivers". Two harmonicas were required for the regular style of Cross Harp playing, and two more for some full chords at the end of the piece where there wasn't time to set the first two down, and pick up the other two. It looked like this.

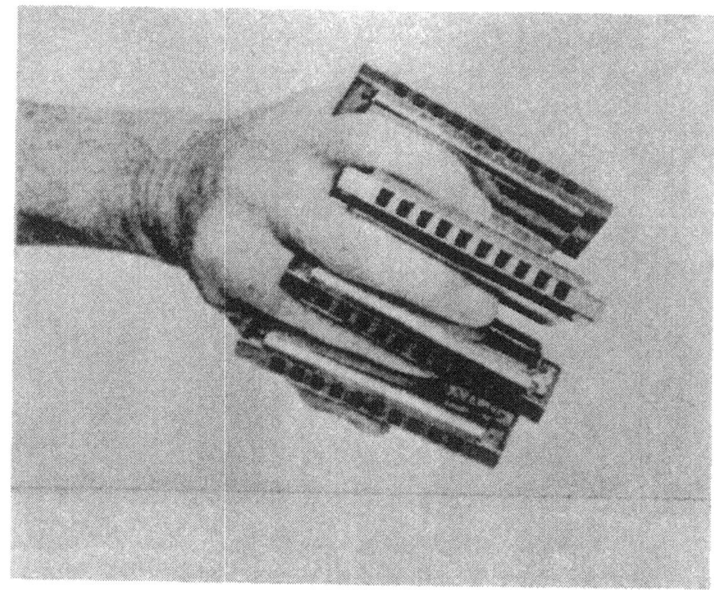

One of the music cues from the motion picture "The Reivers".

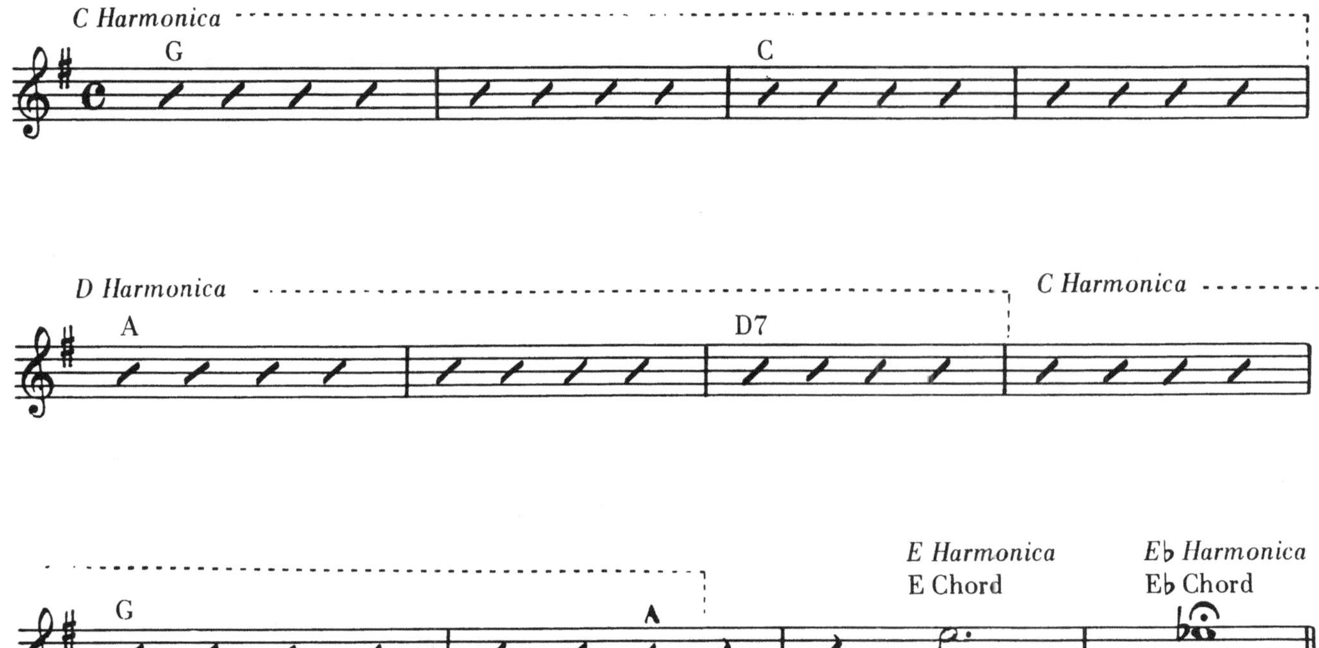

Chapter Eight

Country Music

"Country" as a style of music means many things. The early beginnings have been referred to as hillbilly or cowboy (actually meaning slightly different things). I combine them here to mean the style we think of as solo playing around the campfire or the square dance style of almost 100 years ago. The most important feature of this type of playing is the use of a chord accompaniment while playing the melody. Let's start with the melody "Oh Susanna", Key of C/C Harmonica, Straight Harp:

CHORD STYLE. Played mostly Straight Harp, but occasionally Cross Harp First Position is used. Use Tongue Blocking to play a single tone. To add the chord, lift the tongue from the mouthpiece. To stop the chord, replace the tongue on the mouthpiece. Lifting and replacing the tongue sharply gives a nice attack and cut-off to the accompanying chords. There should be no break or pulse to the melody note. It should remain clear and pure.

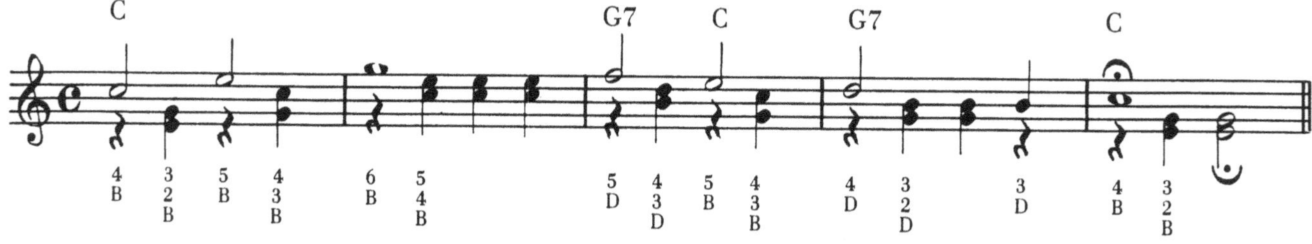

Now let's try "Oh Susanna" again, this time in chord accompaniment style.

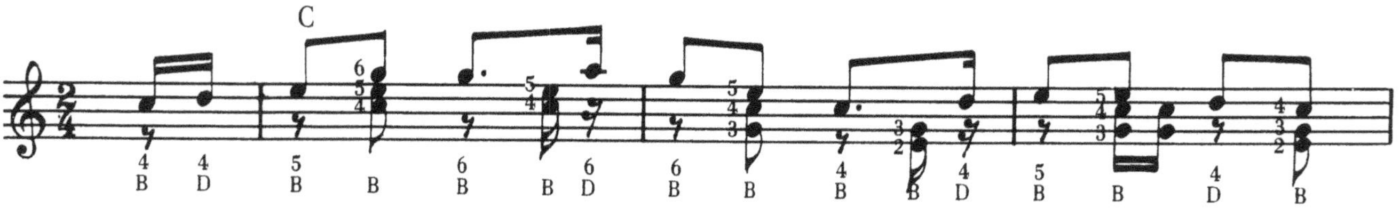

Not all of the notes of the added chords always "fit" the chords of the song. When they don't fit, don't add the accompaniment. Just play the single note at those places. Notice where we left out some of the chords in the middle of "Oh Susanna".

Chord Style is used extensively in the faster tunes, but should be used sparingly when playing slower tempos.

COUNTRY MUSIC TODAY. There are two main styles in today's Country Music.There is the music of smaller groups more closely associated with the style of several years ago, and there is the newer "Pop" Country Music. This "uptown" Country uses large orchestras, more complex melodies, and chords that were unheard of in Country playing a few short years ago. The Chromatic Harmonica is used in this "Pop" Country style to play single note melodies or fills. The Diatonic Harmonica is used for the "other" Country style, known for its simple chords, basic rhythm patterns, and usually associated with smaller bands and groups.

As is the case with blues playing, you must listen to what is happening around you, and fit in with the other players. Use hand vibrato, and some bending, but much less than in blues.

A solo, Key of C/C Harmonica — Straight Harp.

Background (for vocal or guitar lead) – Key of G/C Harmonica – Cross Harp First Position.

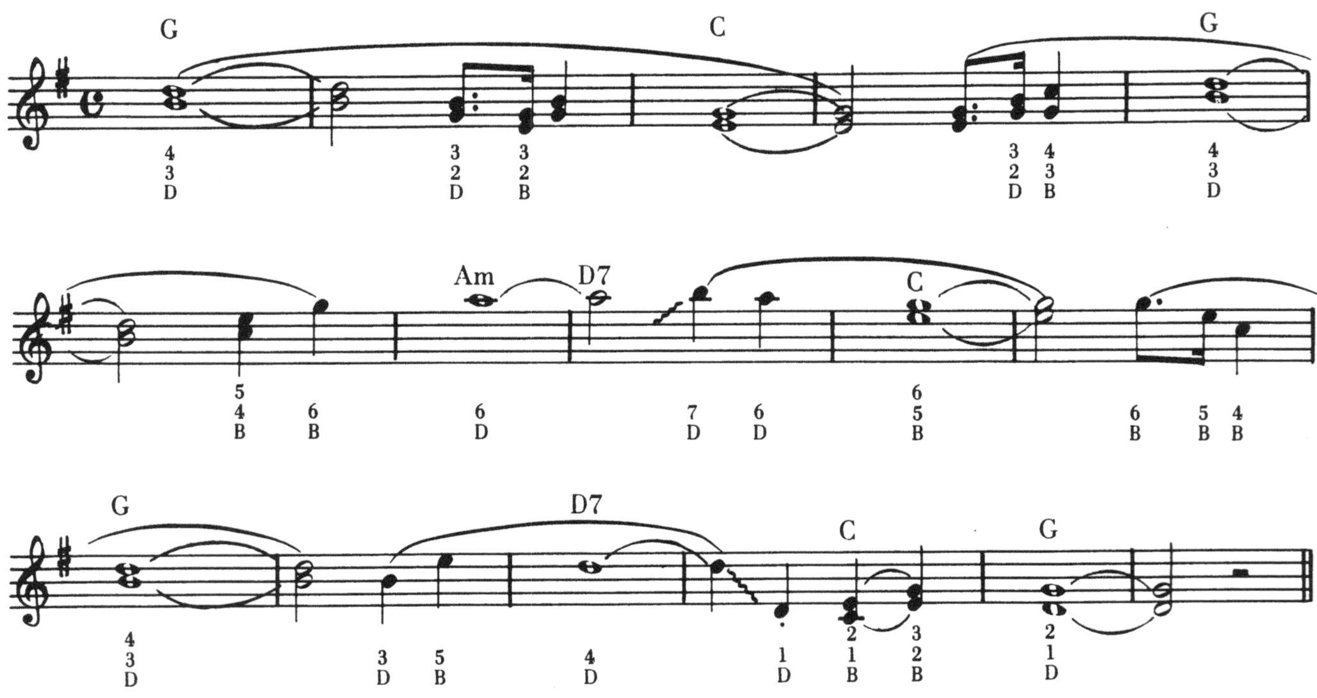

Some of the very fast and brilliant harmonica solos are taken from the "fiddlers", (country violin players). The following is a typical example: Key of G/C Harmonica — Cross Harp First Position.

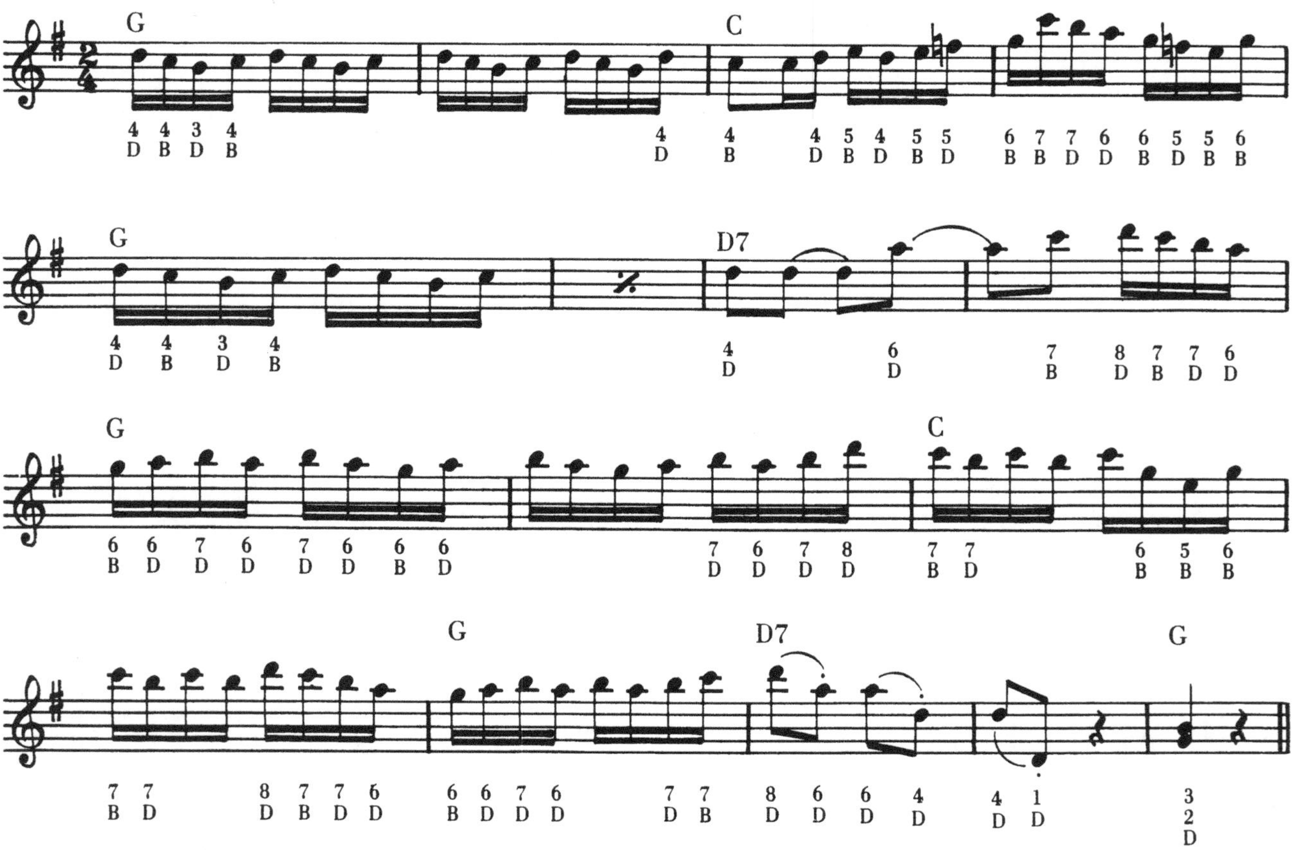

Chapter Nine

Soaking The Harmonica In Water

When played, the harmonica leaks some air from around the tone chambers. Soaking it in water before playing causes the wood in the body to swell and become better seated against the metal reed plates. This condition gives you a much more positive sound, and you will be able to play louder and to bend the notes farther and easier. A small problem can develop if the wood swells above the mouthpiece: it is sharp, and can irritate the lips and tongue. To fix this, simply cut or file the protruding pieces. Be sure to cut or file *across* the mouthpiece, being careful not to let the pieces fall down inside the instrument. It is best to lay the harmonica flat or to hold it upside down to keep a minimum of chips from falling inside where they could possibly jam the reeds.

Chapter Ten

The Electric Harmonica

The use of the electric harmonica grew with the need to be heard in large halls and in outdoor locations. In early days, the sound systems provided at these locations were quite inadequate, as are many even today.

There are some packaged electric pickups available for the Diatonic Harmonica. These are usually attached to the instrument, or the harmonica is inserted into the pick-up, which itself is larger. These packaged pick-ups consist simply of an assembly which mechanically attaches a microphone to the harmonica. When using such a device, take care when playing since *any* noise you make will be transmitted to the microphone through the harmonica and/or the attaching mechanism itself.

The best solution for amplifying your instrument is to use the simple but very effective method of holding a microphone in one hand and playing the harmonica directly into it.

APPENDIX A

Straight Harp and Cross Harp Positions for All Keys

To find which harmonica to use for a particular Major or Minor key, find the heading for the type of playing you wish to do (Straight Harp, Cross Harp First Position, etc.) and look across to the key of the harmonica that appears under the Major Key or Minor Key heading in which you wish to play. For example, to play Straight Harp in the key of A Major, you would use an A Harmonica (the first key listed). For Cross Harp First Position, key of A Major, use a D Harmonica. To be sure you understand what to do, look up the following examples and see if we agree.

Cross Harp Second Position ..... Key of E♭ Major ...... C♯ Harmonica
Straight Harp................. Key of F Minor ...... F Harmonica
Cross Harp Third Position .... Key of C Minor ...... G♯ Harmonica
Cross Harp Fourth Position....... Key of A♭ Minor ...... A Harmonica

MAJOR KEYS	A	Bb	B	C	C♯ (D♭)	D	E♭	E	F	F♯ (G♭)	G	A♭
Key of Harmonica												
Straight Harp	A	Bb	B	C	C♯	D	E♭	E	F	F♯	G	G♯
Cross Harp *1st Position*	D	E♭	E	F	F♯	G	G♯	A	Bb	B	C	C♯
Cross Harp *2nd Position*	G	G♯	A	Bb	B	C	C♯	D	E♭	E	F	F♯
Cross Harp *3rd Position*	F	F♯	G	G♯	A	Bb	B	C	C♯	D	E♭	E

MINOR KEYS	A	Bb	B	C	C♯	D	D♯ (E♭)	E	F	F♯	G	G♯ (A♭)
Key of Harmonica												
Straight Harp	A	Bb	B	C	C♯	D	E♭	E	F	F♯	G	G♯
Cross Harp *1st Position*	C	C♯	D	E♭	E	F	F♯	G	G♯	A	Bb	B
Cross Harp *2nd Position*	G	G♯	A	Bb	B	C	C♯	D	E♭	E	F	F♯
Cross Harp *3rd Position*	F	F♯	G	G♯	A	Bb	B	C	C♯	D	E♭	E
Cross Harp *4th Position*	Bb	B	C	C♯	D	E♭	E	F	F♯	G	G♯	A

APPENDIX B

Basic Music Notation

This section should be used as your music dictionary.

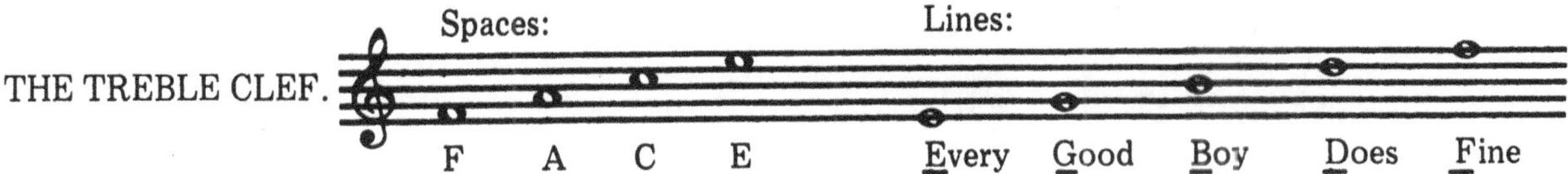

Ledger lines extend the range of the staff (the basic 5 lines and 4 spaces).

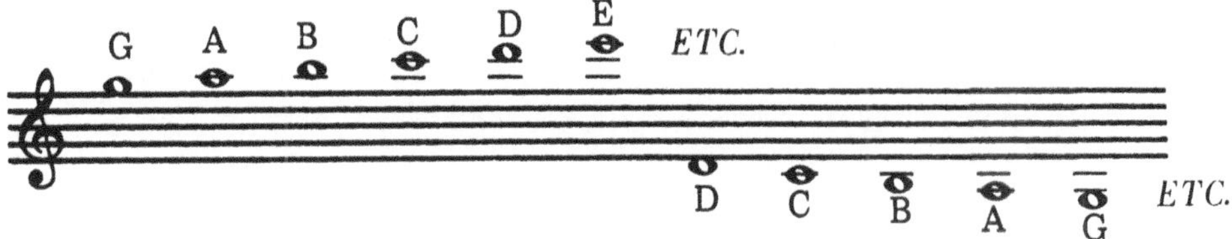

Sharps and Flats

♯ : Sharp. In front of a note means to raise all of those same notes within that measure one half step.

♭ : Flat. In front of a note means to lower all of those same notes within that measure one half step.

♮ : Natural Sign. In front of a note means to cancel the sharp or flat of the key signature for that note or to cancel the sharp or flat that was used in front of the same note earlier in the measure.

Notes and Rests

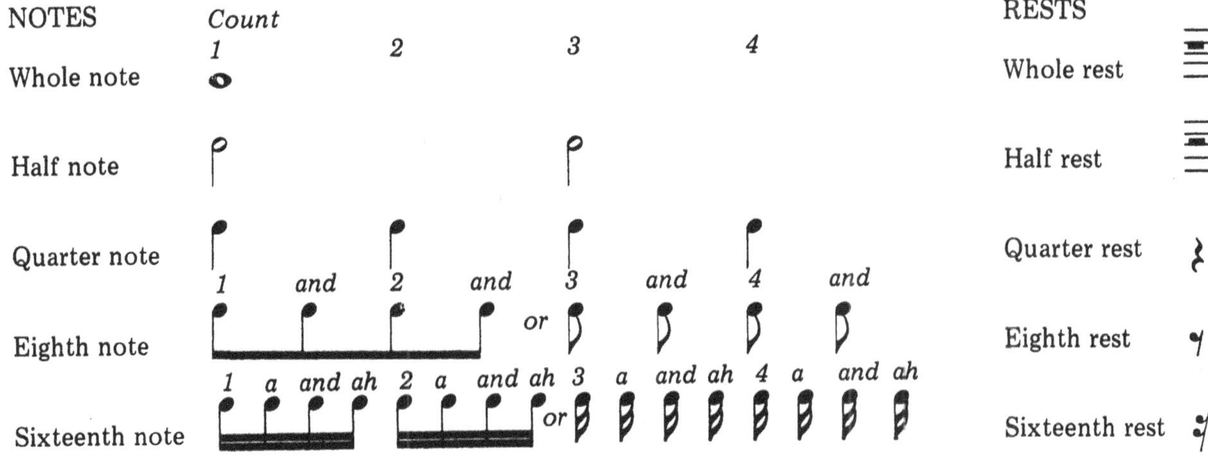

Time in Music

Time signature.

Top number tells the number of beats in each measure or bar of music.

Bottom number tells the note value of each beat.

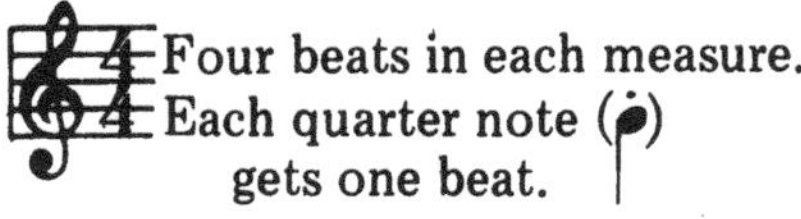

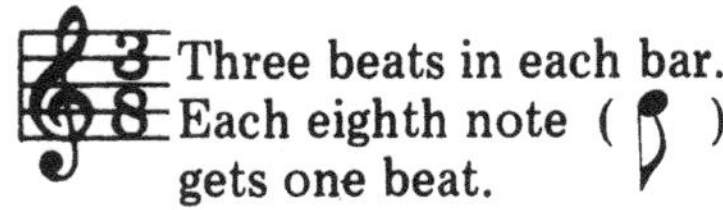

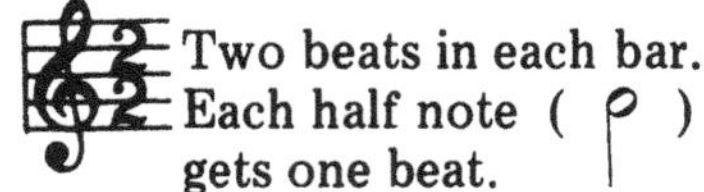

Key Signatures

The number and placement of the Sharps (♯) and Flats (♭) in the staff at the beginning of a piece tell which notes are to be played as a Sharp Note or a Flat Note throughout the entire piece.

The number of Sharps or Flats tells us what key the piece is in (what the tonic note is). Each major key has a relative minor key using the same signature.

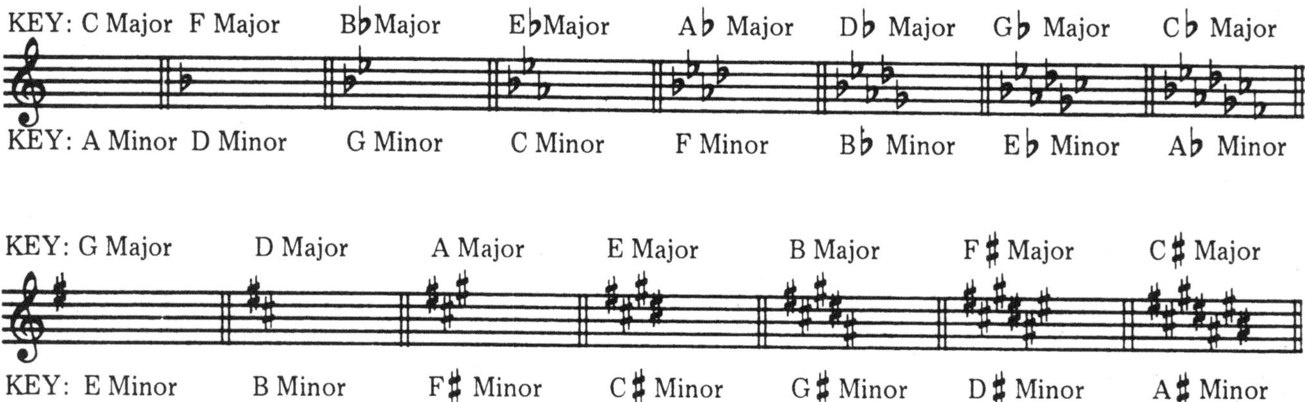

All keys are considered major unless followed by the word minor. Key of C Major is called Key of C,or just C. Key of C minor is called Key of C Minor or C Minor.